The Methuen
Audition Book for Men

Annika Bluhm is herself an actress and
worked for one year, at French's Bookshop,
prior to training at the Guildhall School of
Music and Drama. In the course of
compiling this collection of fifty audition
speeches from some of our finest
contemporary playwrights, she
interviewed a number of directors from
small companies to major institutions. She
has also compiled and edited The Methuen
Audition Book for Women.

The Methuen Audition Book for Men

Compiled by
ANNIKA BLUHM

Methuen Drama

First published in Great Britain in 1989 by Methuen Drama
an imprint of Reed International Books Limited
Michelin House, 81 Fulham Road, London SW3 6RB
and Auckland, Melbourne, Singapore and Toronto
and distributed in the United States of America
by Heinemann, a division of Reed Publishing (USA) Inc,
361 Hanover Street, Portsmouth, New Hampshire NH 03801 3959
Reprinted 1990, 1991 (twice), 1993 (twice), 1994, 1995

A CIP catalogue record for this book is available
from the British Library.

ISBN 0 413 62300 9

Typeset by Hewer Text Composition Services, Edinburgh
Printed and bound in Great Britain by Cox & Wyman Ltd, Reading, Berks

ACKNOWLEDGEMENTS
Grateful acknowledgement is made for permission to reprint extracts from copyrighted
material:

Accrington Pals by Peter Whelan; copyright © 1984, Methuen Drama. **After Haggerty** by David
Mercer; copyright © 1978, Methuen Drama. **Amadeus** by Peter Shaffer; copyright © 1981, Andre
Deutsch Ltd, 105–106 Great Russell Street, London WC1 3LJ and Michael Bessie, 10 East 53rd Street,
Harper and Rowe, New York 10022. **The Art of Success** by Nick Dear; copyright © 1989, Methuen
Drama. **Barbarians** by Barry Keeffe; copyright © 1983, Methuen Drama. **Being Friends** by Robert
Holman; copyright © 1987, Methuen Drama. **Bloody Poetry** by Howard Brenton; copyright © 1985,
Methuen Drama. **The Body** by Nick Darke; copyright © 1981, Methuen Drama. **Class Enemy** by
Nigel Williams; copyright © 1987, Methuen Drama. **Gosforth's Film** from **Confusions** by Alan
Ayckbourn; copyright © 1973, Methuen Drama. **The Conquest of the South Pole** by Manfred Karge;
copyright © 1988, Methuen Drama. **Cries From The Mammal House** by Terry Johnson; copyright ©
1984, Methuen Drama. **Les Mains Sales** (in *The Assassins* trans. Frank Hauser) by Jean-Paul Sartre;
copyright © 1961, Eric Glass, 28 Berkeley Square, W1. **Faith Healer** by Brian Friel; copyright © 1980,
Faber and Faber Ltd, 3 Queen Square, London WC1 3AU. **Family Voices** by Harold Pinter; copyright ©
1981, Methuen Drama. **Fire Raisers** by Max Frisch; copyright © 1961, Suhrkamp Verlag, Frankfurt
am Main. **The Genius** by Howard Brenton; copyright © 1983, Methuen Drama. **Good** by C. P. Taylor;
copyright © 1983, Methuen Drama. **The Great White Hope** by Howard Sackler; copyright © 1987,
Faber and Faber Ltd, 3 Queen Square, London WC1 3AU and Lucy Kroll Agency, 390 West End
Avenue, New York, NY 10024. **Harry's Christmas** by Steven Berkoff; copyright © 1985, Faber and
Faber, 3 Queen Square, London WC1 3AU and Grove Press, 920 Broadway, New York, NY 10010, USA.
Insignificances by Terry Johnson; copyright © 1982, Methuen Drama. **The Lucky Ones** by Tony
Marchant; copyright © 1983, Methuen Drama. **Massage** by Michael Wilcox; copyright © 1983,
Methuen Drama. **Master Harold And The Boys** by Athol Fugard; copyright © 1983, Oxford
University Press, Walton Street, Oxford OX2 6DP. **Maydays** by David Edgar; copyright © 1983,
Methuen Drama. **Moving Pictures** by Stephen Lowe; copyright © 1983, Methuen Drama. **The
Normal Heart** by Larry Kramer; copyright © 1987, Methuen Drama and Margaret Ramsay Ltd, 14a
Goodwin's Court, St Martin's Lane, London WC2N 4LL. **Not Quite Jerusalem** by Paul Kember;
copyright © 1982, Methuen Drama. **Green Forms** from **Office Suite** by Alan Bennett; copyright ©
1981, Faber and Faber Ltd, 3 Queen Square, London WC1 3AU. **One For The Road** by Willy Russell;
copyright © 1988, Methuen Drama. **Our Country's Good** by Timberlake Wertenbaker; copyright ©
1988, Methuen Drama. **The Power of the Dog** by Howard Barker; copyright © 1985, John Calder
(Publishers) Ltd, 18 Brewer Street, London W1R 4AS. **Quaint Honour** by Roger Gellert. Published in
Grays Plays II (ed. Michael Wilcox); copyright © 1986, Methuen Drama. **Rut in the Skull** by Ron
Hutchinson; copyright © 1983, Methuen Drama. **The Real Thing** by Tom Stoppard; copyright ©
1982, Faber and Faber, 3 Queen Square, London WC1 3AU. **Rents** by Michael Wilcox; copyright © 1983,
Methuen Drama. **Road** by Jim Cartwright; copyright © 1988, Methuen Drama. **The Sea** by Edward
Bond; copyright © 1973, Methuen Drama. **Seachange** by Stephen Lowe; copyright © 1985, Methuen
Drama. **Serious Money** by Caryl Churchill; copyright © 1987, Methuen Drama. **Spell #7** by Ntozake
Shange; copyright © 1986, Methuen Drama and St Martin's Press Inc., 175 Fifth Avenue, New York NY
10010. **Stuttgart** by Graham Swannell; copyright © Judy Daish Assoc., 83 Eastbourne Mews, London
W2. **The Suicide** by Nicholai Erdman; copyright © 1979, Methuen Drama. **Teendreams** by David
Edgar and Susan Todd; copyright © 1979, Methuen Drama. **Thatcher's Women** by Kay Adshead.
Published in *Plays by Women VII* (ed. Mary Remnant); copyright © Curtis Brown, 162–168 Regent St.,
London W1. **Translations** by Brian Friel; copyright © 1981, Faber and Faber Ltd, 3 Queen Square,
London WC1 3AU. **Trial Run** by Nigel Williams; copyright © 1983, Methuen Drama. **Tuesday's Child**
by Terry Johnson and Kate Lock; copyright © 1987, Methuen Drama. **Welcome House** by Tony
Marchant; copyright © 1983, Methuen Drama. **Woza Albert** by Mtwa/Ngema/Simon; copyright ©
1983, Methuen Drama.

Contents

Author's Acknowledgements

I would like to thank the following people for all their help, encouragement and advice during the compilation of this book: Lucy Alexander, Annie Castledine, Rachel Cooke, Lindsey Coulson, John Cullen, Richard Eyre, Vanessa Fielding, Powell Jones, Teresa McElroy, Johnathan Petherbridge, Virginia Snyders and Erika Spotswoode.

My special thanks to Jonathan Dow and Emma Rice who had to put up with more tantrums, sulks and general bad behaviour than anyone should have to and wearily accepted my opening gambit of 'What do you think of this speech . . . ?' every time.

And thank you to Pamela Edwardes, Peggy Butcher and Linda Brandon who bemusedly watched me bounce around the Methuen office for the entire summer and only occasionally asked me gently if I was actually working.

This book is the result of a Christmas conversation in Toronto and is therefore for my parents who believe anything is possible.

Annika Bluhm
Derby
1989

Introduction

In the course of compiling this book I spoke to a number of
directors working in various areas of theatre, from drama
schools to the National Theatre. Nearly everyone agreed that
an actor's most important attribute was self-knowledge.
Self-knowledge can be expressed in a variety of ways: through
wit, intelligence, verbal and physical dexterity, an assertive, as
opposed to an aggressive manner.

There is a great difference in approach to auditioning in Britain
and the United States. In America cut-throat competition has
engendered a highly professional attitude. Actors tend to arrive
fully prepared for an audition, on time, with well-rehearsed
speeches from plays that they have taken the time to read in
their entirety. In contrast directors spoke about the appalling
diffidence of many actors in Britain, who arrived in no way
prepared, appearing to feel that the audition was something of
an imposition and that performing was the last thing in the
world they wanted to do.

Directors were keen to emphasize the fact that an audition is not
a test but a meeting between the actor and director to assess the
possibility of working together. Many felt that auditioning
should be more of a two-way process and that actors should
accept more power or responsibility for themselves when
auditioning. In other words, actors should not be tempted to
play down their own intelligence, to act according to what they
think the director wants, but to see themselves as professionals.

Opinions differ as to how much an actor can show about the
way he/she works in an audition. One felt that it was a genuine
opportunity for an actor to display their work; another, that
little could actually be revealed by the presentation of a speech –
auditioning being an artificial performing situation – and that

the actor should concentrate on presenting *themselves* as well as possible, on maximizing their presence. Clearly in an ideal audition one should do both. One should be clear, concise and, equally important, unpretentious. One director talked of avoiding the temptation to be arch. Another was looking for 'assurance with natural reticence', which she went on to explain as including the director in the audition in an open way, talking with, rather than at, him or her.

Most key points as regards the selection and presentation of the audition piece are common sense, but easy to overlook in the attempt to impress. For instance it would be unwise to attempt a speech using a particular accent unless it was well within your capabilities and it would be sensible to choose a role within your own age-range. In the event of an audition being for a specific role, select a pertinent piece: if the production is to be a comedy, present a comic speech. It should be emphasized that there is no substitute, when preparing an audition speech, for reading the play in its entirety.

Everybody acknowledged the advantages of doing a witty or comic piece mainly because they enjoyed being able to laugh. They felt that it was extremely hard for an actor to play a highly emotional scene in an audition without resorting to a good deal of tension, both physically and vocally.

How can you make auditioning a less nerve-racking affair? Most directors agreed on this. Get a good night's sleep, wear comfortable clothes, arrive early and find a quiet place to calm down and 'centre' yourself. Above all, everyone stressed, *have fun*!

Three women factory workers in Manchester are made redundant. They come to London to try and make Christmas money working as prostitutes.

Stan befriends one of the women, Norah, who occupies her day standing around Euston Station. If Stan is aware that she is working as a prostitute he never mentions it. Stan has a gentle, shy and delicate quality. Here he is talking to Norah having taken her back to his room.

Thatcher's Women *by Kay Adshead*

Stan I used to work for pest control, you know, years ago. At Smithfield Market. I'd just come to London, it was the hottest summer in fifteen years – rats were eating the carcasses . . . eating the profits, I suppose. They hired four of us to help out their regular bloke, Thompson. They had guidelines you know, do's and don'ts, but he got bored quickly did Thompson – and he had ideas of his own. One night he decided he was going to smoke out the 'filthy little bastards'. We were in the big stone cellar. Thompson blocked all the passages leading up to the warehouse except one and built a fire of sacking and straw in the corner. We waited at the bottom end of the passage. When they came running out we had to throw cat-gut nets over them and then beat at them with these wooden truncheons. (. . .)

Have you ever seen an animal cornered, Norah? (. . .)

It was terrible. Rats when they panic, scream like – well, like children . . . we'd all been drinking. The other lads were laughing – almost hysterical, swigging back bottles of beer, red faced . . . breathless – all the time hammering down the truncheons on the . . . squirming black mass in the cat-gut net. . . . In the end there must have been one left alive. We were ready to drop with the drink and the smoke, but Thompson hadn't finished yet. He took it out of the net, jammed it against a wall with an old fireguard, he got a kettle of boiling water and poured it over the creature's scabby tail, watching it squeal and jump. Then he got matches, lit them and poked them into the thing's belly, egged another on to stub out his cigarette on the thing's greasy head, watching the fur singe and sizzle . . . with a meat hook they raked the creature's back till they drew dirty black blood. . . . (*Pause.*)

I think after that they must have got bored. They went into the boiler room to play cards. . . . (*Pause.*)

For a while we watched each other – the rat-catcher and the rat . . . I took the fireguard away and put my foot under the thing's backside. 'Go on,' I said. 'Shoo, shoo.' It didn't move. 'Go on,' I said, 'quick, before they come back. You won't get another chance.' Still it didn't move. . . . At last he scampered to the door. Then, suddenly, before turning into the passage, it stopped and looked at me straight in the eye, a long slow stare from clever pink eyes as if to say . . .

He laughs, half embarrassed – half upset.

'Thanks. Thanks, Stan.'

Stuttgart is one of a series of playlets examining marriage and adultery in the modern day. In this short piece a married couple reveal their very different attitudes towards sex. In this speech Terence is rehearsing an imaginary conversation in the mirror with his wife, Caroline, in which he suggests that they could make love less often.

Stuttgart (from **A State of Affairs**)
by Graham Swannell

Terence No, these days, I can't get away from my first thought, when I hear you say with that particular look in your eye, when you say, Are you coming up, Terence? Well, my first thought is, Caroline, oh, Christ! Do we really have to?

I mean, I'm a regular fellow, but recently, well, it just doesn't excite me. God knows why.

I used to be, well, you know me. Any time. Day or night. Any time and more than once. Many times more than once. Even I amazed myself sometimes. I thought, you're bloody amazing you are. You even said I was amazing. With good reason. That was me. Any time.

I don't know what's happened to me. I look at my watch and think, bloody hell, it's nearly ten-thirty! Bloody hell! I'll be at it within the hour. Or there I am sitting in my armchair, quietly reading in my armchair, when up you pop from behind the chair and start kissing me with your tongue. Well . . . your tongue. Actually there's nothing left to document about your tongue. I mean, there I am reading my Maupassant short stories when this 'Tongue' is thrust into my mouth. It is virtually down my throat. I'm on the point of choking I am. My head is crushed against the back of the chair and I'm supposed to cast aside my Maupassant and it's off with the old clothes and down on the carpet we go!

It's not as if we haven't done it before. It's not some new discovery. We have done it before. God knows how many times we've done it before.

Brief pause.

Well, it must be quite a few times. It's probably running into thousands of times. It's been what? Since . . . '69, well . . . that's quite a few thousand times isn't it? Well, actually it's bloody thousands of times! So it's safe to say, We know what it's like!

Somehow I've got off the point. What is the point?

The point is, Caroline, if we did it less, if we made love less, I think it might help me. I think it might help me regain my appetite.

How less?

Well, the figure that springs to mind. If we agreed to do it less. The figure that springs. Is . . . um . . . once a month. Yes. Once a month. What do you think?

She'll destroy me!

Green Forms is a farce set in a small department of a large office organization. All the workers ignore the politics of their jobs but are dominated by the red tape of the organization for which they work.

Lomax is a one-armed Northerner. He is the office messenger, loathed by the women in the office. In this speech he has burst into the office delivering supplies. He totally ignores the women and only talks to his young assistant.

Green Forms (from **Office Suite**)
by Alan Bennett

Lomax   I said 'ASTMS?' He said 'Yes.' I said 'I've always assumed I
was Transport and General Workers.' 'A common mistake' he said.
Nice looking feller. Bit of a beard. Only young. I said 'ASTMS? That's
Scientific, Technical and Managerial.' 'Mr Lomax,' he said (he knew
my name), 'full marks.' I said 'Well, for a kick-off I'm not Scientific.
Furthermore I am not Technical, and in addition I am not
Managerial.' He said 'Excuse me, friend, but haven't I seen you
adjusting the thermostat for the central heating?' I said 'That is one of
my functions.' 'Right' he said 'You're Scientific. Don't you on
occasions man the lift?' 'Manually operated in cases of emergency, yes
I do.' 'Right' he said 'you're Technical.' 'Do you have access to a
telephone?' I said 'Yes.' 'Right' he said 'you're Managerial.' 'Frank,'
he said (he knew my name), 'you shouldn't be in the TGWU, you. You,
Frank, are hard-core ASTMS. You are what we call an ancillary
worker.' I said 'Naturally, I shall want time to study this one out.
You're probably a political person. I vote, but that's about as far as it
goes. Furthermore,' I said (I put my cards on the table), 'furthermore,
I've frequently had occasion to vote Conservative.' 'Don't apologize,
Frank' he said. 'It's a free country.' 'Whereas you,' I said, 'I don't
know, but I imagine, just looking at you (and I don't mean the earring;
my eldest lad wears one, married with a nice little milk-round in
Doncaster) you are . . . probably a militant.' 'Up to a point, Frank' he
said. 'Yes.' So I said, 'Well let's get it quite straight at the outset, I have
no sympathy for that at all. I fought in the Western Desert and I have
no sympathy for that at all.' He went very quiet. He said, 'Frank. Let
me ask you one question. Pay and Conditions. Satisfied or not
satisfied?' 'Not satisfied,' I said. 'Nor are we,' he said! *'Nor are we.'* 'Can
I ask you another question? Are you index linked?' 'Alas,' I said, 'No.'
'Top of the agenda, Frank' he said. 'Our No. 1 priority.' So I said,
'What about comparable facilities? TGWU has a very nice holiday
home at Cleveleys.' He said, 'Have you ever been to Mablethorpe?' No.
'Frank,' he said, 'you're got a treat in store.'

Our Country's Good takes as its basis the performance of Farquhar's *The Recruiting Officer* by a cast of convicts in Australia in 1789.

Ketch Freeman is a convict who has accepted the post of hangman and as such is hated and feared by the rest of the community. He hopes to be cast in the play and thereby gain popularity. He has come to beg the officer casting the play for a part.

Our Country's Good
by Timberlake Wertenbaker

Ketch James, Sir, James, Daniel, Patrick, after my three uncles.
Good men they were too, didn't go to London. If my mother hadn't
brought us to London, may God give peace to her soul and breathe pity
into the hearts of hard women – because the docks are in London and if
I hadn't worked on the docks, on that day, May 23rd, do you remember
it, Sir? Shadwell Dock. If only we hadn't left, then I wouldn't have been
there, then nothing would have happened, I wouldn't have become a
coal heaver on Shadwell Dock and been there on the 23rd of May when
we refused to unload because they were paying us so badly Sir. I wasn't
even near the sailor who got killed. He shouldn't have done the
unloading, that was wrong of the sailors, but I didn't kill him, maybe
one blow, not to look stupid, you know, just to show I was with the lads,
even if I wasn't, but I didn't kill him. And they caught five at random
Sir, and I was among the five, and they found the cudgel, but I just had
that to look good, that's all, and when they said to me later you can
hang or you can give the names what was I to do, what would you have
done, Sir?

Ralph I wouldn't have been in that situation, Freeman.

Ketch To be sure, forgive me, Sir. I only told on the ones I saw. I
didn't tell anything that wasn't true, death is a horrible thing, that poor
sailor.

I understand, Sir, I understand. And when it happened again, here!
And I had hopes of making a good life here. It's because I'm so friendly,
see, so I go along, and then I'm the one who gets caught, that theft, I
didn't do it, I was just there, keeping a look out, just to help some
friends, you know. But when they say to you, hang or be hanged, what
do you do? Someone has to do it. I try to do it well. God have mercy on
the whore, the thief, the lame, surely he'll forgive me? – it's the women –
they're without mercy – not like you and me, Sir, men. What I wanted
to say, Sir, is that I heard them talking about the play.

Pause.

Some players came into our village once, they were loved like the
angels, Lieutenant, like the angels. And the way the women watched
them – the light of a spring dawn in their eyes.

Lieutenant.

I want to be an actor.

9

Hally is a white South African boy whose closest friends are the two black men who work for his family. The news of his alcoholic father's return home from hospital upsets Hally, causing him to turn against his two old friends. The play shows how the closest relationships can be distorted by the pressures of society and the political situation.

Master Harold . . . and the boys
by Athol Fugard

Hally   It started off looking like another of those useless
nothing-to-do afternoons. I'd already been down to Main Street
looking for adventure, but nothing had happened. I didn't feel like
climbing trees in the Donkin Park or pretending I was a private eye and
following a stranger . . . so as usual: See what's cooking in Sam's room.
This time it was you on the floor. You had two thin pieces of wood and
you were smoothing them down with a knife. It didn't look particularly
interesting, but when I asked you what you were doing, you just said,
'Wait and see, Hally. Wait . . . and see' . . . in that secret sort of way of
yours, so I knew there was a surprise coming. You teased me, you
bugger, by being deliberately slow and not answering my questions!

Sam laughs.

And whistling while you worked away! God, it was infuriating! I could
have brained you! It was only when you tied them together in a cross and
put that down on the brown paper that I realized what you were doing.
'Sam is making a kite?' And when I asked you and you said 'Yes' . . . !

(Shaking his head with disbelief.) The sheer audacity of it took my breath
away. I mean, seriously, what the hell does a black man know about
flying a kite? I'll be honest with you, Sam, I had no hopes for it. If you
think I was excited and happy, you got another guess coming. In fact, I
was shit-scared that we were going to make fools of ourselves. When we
left the boarding house to go up onto the hill, I was praying quietly that
there wouldn't be any other kids around to laugh at us. (. . .) You went
a little distance from me down the hill, you held it up ready to let it
go. . . . 'This is it,' I thought. 'Like everything else in my life, here comes
another fiasco.' Then you shouted, 'Go, Hally!' and I started to run.
(Another pause.)

I don't know how to describe it, Sam. Ja! The miracle happened! I was
running, waiting for it to crash to the ground, but instead suddenly
there was something alive behind me at the end of the string, tugging at
it as if it wanted to be free. I looked back . . .

(Shakes his head.) . . . I still can't believe my eyes. It was flying! Looping
around and trying to climb even higher into the sky. You shouted to me
to let it have more string. I did, until there was none left and I was just
holding that piece of wood we had tied it to. You came up and joined
me. You were laughing.

After the Falklands War a detachment of Paras return to England for the military burial of one of their platoon. Gradually the soldiers begin to react against the jingoism surrounding the war, as they find themselves less able to rationalize or make sense of Kilby's death.

Polo, dangerously close to cracking, avoids his memories through an obsession with pop groups. He is talking to another member of the troop, who is sharing his bunk, on the night before the funeral.

Welcome Home *by Tony Marchant*

Polo   Goldy? (...)

Did I tell you that Depêche Mode might be splitting up? (...)

Be a shame if they did – I really liked their first LP – what's your favourite single of theirs? *Leave in Silence* is mine. (...)

They come from Basildon. Did you know? (...)

Funny name innit – Depêche Mode. It's French. (...)

I just thought – you might want to talk. (...)

I don't want to dream. (...)

Reminders . . . y'know . . . coming in me head. Kilby's hair flying about in the wind and the hole in his neck. I saw him . . . he was dead but his hair was moving . . . fell just below this ridge . . . and still nowhere near Boca Hill. Didn't know what to do . . . too scared to cry, wished I'd been in one of the other companies. Someone was shouting at me to get his belt . . . for the rounds it had left. I still hear the way he cried out and the noise of the mortars and the pucaras coming through the anchorage. Sometimes I hear 'em louder than other times – I brought 'em home with me – it's like they're stretching inside me head till there's no room left. Only thing worse is the quiet in between. The quiet was when we was waiting. When we had to wait – for the quiet to stop. I love records – they're normal. They're always on. Am I talking like a pratt Goldy? (...)

Kilby stopped hearing, stopped being scared. Just his hair moving in the wind. I dream about him . . . what a sniper did. And when the doors of the school house were opened – all the bodies . . . like the charred wood on a burnt out bonfire. All black and twisted together. Not like real people.And now we've got to bury Terry again. I was thinking, before it started, that it'd be a bit like going on exercise.

Pause.

I stuck a bayonet in one of their bellies. It made a sort of gurgling sound. I had its blood on me bayonet. I think I killed it. I just behaved y'know. Stay awake with us Goldy.

Rikki is a nineteen-year-old masseur. He arrives at the house of Doug ostensibly to give him 'just a massage'. Doug is suspected of having made sexual advances towards his girlfriend's son. As they talk Rikki begins to explain about his childhood and his adoption.

Massage *by Michael Wilcox*

Rikki   When I was ten. The people there, they got me all dressed up 'cause I was going to meet someone who wanted to adopt me. That's what the kids there dreamed of. Someone coming. Someone good . . . you know . . . to take you with them . . . to be your dad . . . take you on holidays and that . . . have your own room and your own things . . . possessions. Anyway, I was in this room and the door opened and this man and woman walked in, and I remember thinking, 'Bloody Hell! I'm not going off with them! The other kids'll think I'm daft!' But I did. Just for the afternoon. You don't clear off for good, just like that. They have to get to know you, to see if they like you. (. . .)

Caught the train to Southend. (. . .)

I'd been there before with the other kids . . . you know . . . from the Home. Seen the Wax Works. 'Torture through the Ages.' Not much cop. Supposed to be educational. Looked at the *Golden Hind*. Went on the racing cars by the pier. Great to be with someone with money to spend. When we was having a day out with the Home, we had to spend a lot of time just watching other kids having fun. Then we went to the Kursaal . . . big dippers and that. But we was running out of money. There was this incredible ride called The Toboggan. So mum and dad and me gets on this sledge thing and start to get hoisted up to the top of the Cresta Run. And once you're on it, there's no escape, even if you have a heart attack on the way up. 'Cause you can't see, when you pays your money, just how steep it is 'cause it goes right out of sight. But on the way up me mum starts screaming and dad's had a few drinks and says he feels sick and I was laughing. And when we gets to the top there's this lad with tattoos like a gipsy and he doesn't take the blindest notice of me dad, who threatens to bottle him. And the next thing we know, we're charging down this vertical run on a wooden tray at a hundred miles an hour. And we all screamed our heads off. And when we got to the top of the next hump, dad threw up and mum lost her hat! And I thought, 'If they can do this for me, maybe they're not so daft.'

Sean is the brother of Teresa who has returned pregnant from a holiday in the Holy Land. She claims that it is an immaculate conception. As the press and tourists flock to their home Sean refuses to be drawn into the religious fervour. He cares deeply for Teresa and becomes an ally to her confused and doubtful priest, to whom he is speaking at this moment.

Tuesday's Child
by Terry Johnson and Kate Lock

Sean You're a better carpenter than I am. But you know, sometimes I think I'd have made a better priest than you. To my mind the best sort of priest is the priest who rolls up his cassock and hits old John Wayne in the eye, or gets it sopping wet salvaging shipwrecked arms for the freedom fighters. Opens Boys' Towns. Gets drunk at weddings and dances with young widows. A bit of fire in him, a bit of spirit, and a touch of hypocrisy when it comes to the ladies. Trevor Howard sort of a priest. That's what I'd be.

Doyle And what sort am I?

Sean Miserable sort. The sort who should have got himself seduced by an older woman on the train to the seminary. Sent a postcard to his mother. 'Dear Ma. Never made it. Bad luck. Thomas.'

Doyle No, she'd have found me.

He takes an indigestion table.

Sean It's given you an ulcer, hasn't it? I know how it feels. I was going to be a computer genius, but once you've learnt how to use that thing the bottom falls right out of the joy of it. Once I'd taught it to do what I told it, I couldn't think of anything worth telling it to do. But I could be a great computer programmer. But then I could be a great chicken farmer too. Or a great priest. But I'd rather not be up to my neck in floppy discs, chicken shit, or Holy wafers. It probably stops you thinking altogether about anything else. Does it?

In a comprehensive school a group of boys are left alone in a classroom waiting for a teacher. They are considered to be 'no-hopers' by authority and their rage and frustration at this situation leads to their holding their own class, each teaching the others something that they can do.

Snatch is black, permanently in trouble with the police and unrepentant of his criminal record. The speech is Snatch's 'lesson'.

Class Enemy *by Nigel Williams*

Snatch Right. Winders.

Pause.

I started on winders when I was in ve ovver school over by ver railway. Some cunt sez ter me in class ''oo you bovverin' nigger?' jus' like that. No one ever called me that before. Nigger. I never 'eard it know what I mean? So I went 'ome I arxt ve ol' lady I sez 'Ma – woss it all abaht viss nigger?' She jus' laughed. But me Dad wuz furious an' 'en vey 'ad a row sayin' one 'fing arter anuvver an' 'fore they finished they as callin' each other nigger an' a lot of uvver 'fings beside. But it was funny. I din't like it. I din't like ver fuckin' word. Nigger. Jus' din't like it. An' I couldn't ferget it. So.

Pause.

I'm goin' ter school nex' day an' I pass vis shop dahn Railton Road. 'Lectrics. Kettles an' 'at an' fires an' all. All clean an' gleamin'. An' in ver middle 'ere's vis lit'l girl, paper cut-out, wiv gaps in 'er front teeth, grinnin' like on ver telly. I stop. I look at vis girl. An' fer some reason I don' like 'er. Iss like this. I'm stuck vere in Railton Road an' everywhere roun' me is black people, black geezers in a' doorways, black girls goin' to an' fro from ver launjrettes and black guys like my ol' man in cars – them square ones – Austin Cambridge they are hundreds a' years old. An' in 'iss winder vere's vis paper cut-out girl an' she's white. I mean so fuckin' white it makes yer sick.

Pause. They're listening to him as never before.

Well I 'fought ter meself 'Fuck you darlin'. 'Cos it was like she was sayin' one 'fing ter me you know? She was sayin' 'nigger' ter me like that kid in the class. There some ovver people in a blow up photo be'ind 'er they was sayin' 'nigger' an' all. They was sayin' 'We got all ve electric kettles an' fires an' anyfing we wants so you fuck off black boy.' So. I picks up vis stone an' chucks it. Warn't big enough. I chucks anuvver. No good. Ven I gess me satchel an' loads it up wiv' stones an' rubbish an' anyfing I can find an' when the road's quiet I swing it round an' round an' then let go – like *that*. Oh. You shoulda seen that glass. Shoulda *seen* it.

Dreamy.

Bes' time fer winders is 'free in ver mornin' when no one's abaht.

The Power of the Dog is set in Eastern Europe amidst the
mayhem of 1945 and the triumphant advance of the Red Army.

Archie McGroot is a Scotsman who has been brought to
Russia to act as Stalin's comedian. He struggles desperately to
find a balance between speaking the truth and staying alive. In
this speech he is practising his juggling techniques whilst
waiting to entertain Stalin. He is talking to himself.

The Power Of The Dog *by Howard Barker*

McGroot The mon tells me this is an honour. Wha' kind of honour, says A, A ha' spent ma life avoidin' honours – the honour o' servin' wi' His Majesty's forces, the honour o' makin' a wooman decent in the eyes o' God, the honour o' buyin' the boss a drink, cheers, but honour's somethin' A can do wi'out. He says, the honour o' bein' the furst Scotsman to appear in the Kremlin. A pretended ta think aboot it – well, ye gotta look serious, haven't ye – an' then A said, wi' all respect, A'm perfectly happy wi' the circus. A've noo great ambition to play the Kremlin, it's noo a billin' A'm so desperate for. But he's very persistent – they can be persistent, can't they – he tells me this is one honour A canna refuse, there's noo exactly a glut o' Scots entertainers in the USSR. A was put on the shortlist – in fact, A was at the top of it – in fact, there was only one name on it – an' he showed it to me, an' there it was – Archie McGroot. A looked at it a minute. Archie McGroot, ma name's Vladimir Galoshev –

Stalin enters, with his Aides. McGroot drops the balls.

– fuck –

He scrambles after them.

A will noo survive this . . . A will noo see the streets o' Paisley underneath ma boots agin, A'm a doomed mon –

He drops the balls again.

Christ . . . !

He retrieves them.

He does noo laugh, it's like flashin' yer bollocks in the convent –

He walks on his hands to where Stalin is idly tasting food.

Wha' did the Emperor say to the clown?

Stalin ignores him.

Wha' did the Emperor say to the clown?

Stalin wanders off.

Fuckin' hell, A should ha' stayed in the clubs, but A'm an idealist . . .

Salieri, the Court Composer to the Emperor of Austria, finds his music mediocre in comparison to that of the young Mozart. Mozart is a buffoon – a seemingly childish, game-playing, raspberry-blowing hysteric who can write the music of the angels. The play shows Salieri's initial disbelief and growing jealousy of Mozart.

Mozart has just entered Salieri's salon, talking excitedly about his ideas for an opera. He has just shocked the men present by declaring that 'all serious operas written this century are boring' and goes on to explain his passion for opera.

Amadeus *by Peter Shaffer*

They turn and look at him in shocked amazement. A pause. He gives his little giggle, and then jumps down again.

Mozart Look at us! Four gaping mouths. What a perfect quartet! I'd love to write it – just this second of time, this *now*, as you are! Herr Chamberlain thinking 'Impertinent Mozart: I must speak to the Emperor at once!' Herr Prefect thinking 'Ignorant Mozart: debasing opera with his vulgarity!' Herr Court Composer thinking 'German Mozart: what can he finally know about music?' And Herr Mozart himself, in the middle, thinking 'I'm just a good fellow. Why do they all disapprove of me?'

*Excitedly to **Van Swieten**.*

That's why opera is important, Baron. Because it's realer than any play! A dramatic poet would have to put all those thoughts down one after another to represent this second of time. The composer can put them all down at once – and still make us hear each one of them. Astonishing device: a Vocal Quartet!

More and more excited.

. . . I tell you I want to write a finale lasting half an hour! A quartet becoming a quintet becoming a sextet. On and on, wider and wider – all sounds multiplying and rising together – and the together making a sound entirely new! . . . I bet you that's how God hears the world. Millions of sounds ascending at once and mixing in His ear to become an unending music, unimaginable to us!

*To **Salieri**.*

That's our job! That's our job, we composers: to combine the inner minds of him and him and him, and her and her – the thoughts of chambermaids and Court Composers – and turn the audience into God.

Family Voices was originally written as a radio piece and shows the relationship between a young man who has left home for the first time and his parents. Voice One is the rather naïve and gullible son. This is his first letter home to his mother.

Family Voices *by Harold Pinter*

Voice One   Do you miss me?

I am having a very nice time and I hope you are glad of that.

At the moment I am dead drunk.

I had five pints in The Fishmongers Arms tonight, followed by three double scotches, and literally rolled home.

When I say home I can assure you that my room is extremely pleasant. So is the bathroom. Extremely pleasant. I have some very pleasant baths indeed in the bathroom. So does everybody else in the house. They all lie quite naked in the bath and have very pleasant baths indeed. All the people in the house go about saying what a superb bath and bathroom the one we share is, they go about telling literally everyone they meet what lovely baths you can get in this place, more or less unparalleled, to put it bluntly.

When I said I was drunk I was of course making a joke.

I bet you laughed.

Mother?

Did you get the joke? You know I never touch alcohol.

I like being in this enormous city, all by myself. I expect to make friends in the not too distant future.

I expect to make girlfriends too.

I expect to meet a very nice girl. Having met her, I shall bring her home to meet my mother.

I get on very well with my landlady, Mrs Withers. She tells me I am her solace. I have a drink with her at lunchtime and another one at teatime and then take her for a couple in the evening at The Fishmongers Arms.

She was in the Women's Air Force in the Second World War. Don't drop a bollock, Charlie, she's fond of saying. Call him Flight Sergeant and he'll be happy as a pig in shit.

You'd really like her, mother.

A young U.S. marine dies on an American airbase and his body goes missing. Set in an eccentric English village community, the play is a black farce centring on the search for the body by the authorities.

The Body appears on stage throughout the play as a corpse and at this point comes alive briefly in order to explain to the audience why he died.

The Body *by Nick Darke*

Body   When I was alive, towards the end of my life – by the way I'm dead right now, I died, close on five minutes ago – I had a fear of yawning. Got to figuring if I yawned too hard the skin round my lips, when they opened wide, would peel right back over my head and down my neck and turn me inside out. I started to yawn when I was sixteen, back home, when I was bored. I know that healthy guys when they hit sixteen start to do things other than yawn. But believe me where I came from there was little hope of that. And yawning was the next best thing. One day my paw caught me yawning. He said, 'Son, join the marines.' (…)

I said, 'Paw I'm bored'. He said, 'The marines will sure kick the shit outa that.' So I enlisted. First thing they do is cut my hair off. Which kinda makes me uneasy cus by now I'd reached neurosis point about this skin peeling business, and I figured the only thing which would stop the skin from shooting right back over the top of my skull when I yawned was the hair. Figured it might like hold it in check long enough for me to yank it all back into place. But on my first day . . . had my head shaved . . . believe me I kept my mouth tight shut. But, by the end of my training at boot camp on Parris Island I was a highly tuned killing machine, prepared to be sent to any part of the world, get shot up and die protecting the free world from the onslaught of Communism. Paw was right. Sure kicked the shit outa yawning. I was ready to kill. Go over the top. I had a weapon in my hand and my finger itched to squeeze the trigger. Got to figure if it itched much more it'd drop off. I had visions of me under fire, storming a tree line in a fire fight and comin' up face to face with a big Soviet stormtrooper and there I am weapon in hand ready to blast the bastard to boot hill finger on the trigger and the damn thing's itchin' so much it drops off. We were issued with ointment anyhow to relieve the . . . er, but, what happens? I'm sent here. Guarding warheads. Sitting on top of that observation tower, which thank Christ was made unsafe by the last gale, and walking up and down the fence, guarding warheads against sheep! I started yawning again. Twice, three times a day. Then it hit me. We were trained to kill, and to die. Now I dunno whether any a you good people are dead, but if you are still alive, the one thing that bothers us about dying is what happens after. I only died five minutes ago but it strikes me being dead is much the same as being alive. It's boring. I think I've bin sent to hell. Don't die. I made a mistake. I erred. It's hell all right. So. I'm dead. And in hell.

The Normal Heart is about the growing danger of the AIDS crisis in New York. Ned is a journalist and one of the most vociferous members of the gay community. His frustration and antagonism grows as the authorities remain indifferent and hostile to the epidemic. Unfortunately for Ned this antagonism leads to his expulsion from the Gay Advice Center which he has helped to establish. Here he is pleading with his friend Bruce to be allowed to continue in his work for AIDS awareness. His plea is rejected and Ned is expelled.

The Normal Heart *by Larry Kramer*

Ned   I belong to a culture that includes Proust, Henry James, Tchaikovsky, Cole Porter, Plato, Socrates, Aristotle, Alexander the Great, Michelangelo, Leonardo da Vinci, Christopher Marlowe, Walt Whitman, Herman Melville, Tennessee Williams, Byron, E. M. Forster, Lorca, Auden, Francis Bacon, James Baldwin, Harry Stack Sullivan, John Maynard Keynes, Dag Hammarskjöld. . . . These were not invisible men. Poor Bruce. Poor frightened Bruce. Once upon a time you wanted to be a soldier. Bruce, did you know that it was an openly gay Englishman who was as responsible as any man for winning the Second World War? His name was Alan Turing and he cracked the German's Enigma code so the Allies knew in advance what the Nazis were going to do – and when the war was over he committed suicide he was so hounded for being gay. Why don't they teach any of this in the schools? If they did, maybe he wouldn't have killed himself and maybe you wouldn't be so terrified of who you are. The only way we'll have real pride is when we demand recognition of a culture that isn't just sexual. It's all there – all through history we've been there; but we have to claim it, and identify who was in it, and articulate what's in our minds and hearts and all our creative contributions to this earth. And until we do that, and until we organize ourselves block by neighbourhood by city by state into a united visible community that fights back, we're doomed. That's how I want to be defined: as one of the men who fought the war. Being defined by our cocks is literally killing us. Must we all be reduced to becoming our own murderers? Why couldn't you and I, Bruce Niles and Ned Weeks, have been leaders in creating a new definition of what it means to be gay? I blame myself as much as you. Bruce, I know I'm an asshole. But, please, I beg you, don't shut me out.

Maydays is a vast play spanning over twenty-five years and showing the fate of the socialist ideal through the eyes of three men, one of them Jeremy.

Over the course of the play Jeremy abandons his youthful communist principles to become a member of the hard right in late middle-age. At this point in the play Jeremy, in his thirties, is a history master at a minor public school. He is speaking to a left-wing schoolboy.

Maydays *by David Edgar*

Jeremy   All right, then. Look, I was born in Halifax. And although my family would not have known an opportunist tendency had one leant over and bit them – in fact they thought that reading stunted growth – we all knew people who had elder brothers, fathers, friends, who were either near or in the Party. And some of them, the very best of them, went off to Spain. And the very best of those did not come back.

And so when *we* came of age, when it was all over, the thirties and the war, we had this feeling we were fifteen years too young. And I tell you, there's no stranger feeling than the feeling that instead of being past it, it's past you.

And what we'd missed, of course, was all the glory. And indeed the confidence, that once you'd cracked the shackles of the system, every man indeed would be an Aristotle or a Michelangelo. Because in a way, it had already happened. And it hadn't turned out how we thought it would at all. Oh, it was decent sure, and reasonably caring, in its bureaucratic way. . . . And indeed there was full employment and high wages and although there was still some miserable poverty, there was less of it than there'd ever been before. . . . And, for us, of course, we did particularly well, there were scholarships, and places at the less pretentious Oxbridge colleges, and some of us wrote poetry, and others novels, and some were published, and some not . . .

And we worked on literary magazines, or the Third Programme, or we didn't . . .

But you realize there's something missing. The working class is freer than it's ever been. But somewhere, in the no-man's-land between private affluence and public squalor, somewhere inside the Hoover Automatic or the Mini-Cooper, behind the television or underneath the gramophone, those wonderful possessions . . . you hear a kind of scream. The scream of the possessed.

And you realize there's all the difference in the world, between liberty and liberation.

31

Good is set in Germany during the thirties and follows the rise of fascism through the eyes of one man.

Halder is a university professor who joins the Nazi Party in order to keep his job and gradually finds himself embroiled deeper and deeper in the fascist movement. From supervising book-burnings to becoming an officer at Auschwitz, Halder continues to regard himself as a good and humane man. He addresses this speech to his increasingly frantic Jewish friend, Maurice, on *Kristallnacht* – a campaign of terror carried out against the Jews in pre-war Germany.

Good *by C. P. Taylor*

Halder   I am not deluding myself . . . am I? Maurice? This is a regime in its childhood . . . It's social experiment in its earliest stages . . . You know what a child is like . . . Self-discipline isn't formed, yet a large element of unpredictability . . . It *could* be . . . if the Jews stayed here much longer . . . You see what I'm getting at . . . ? Some of the extreme elements in the regime, could get out of hand . . . Christ knows *what* they would do to the Jews next . . .

I see tonight . . . As a basically humane action . . . It's going to shock the Jews into the *reality* of their situation in Nazi Germany . . . Tomorrow morning . . . They'll be running for their lives out of the country.

. . . A sharp, sudden shock . . . that is going to make those who still delude themselves they can stay here in peace to face reality . . . and . . .

Keep out of it . . . As much as possible. You can do fuck all about it. Tonight . . . what can I do about it? All over the country, they'll be marching against the Jews.

It's a bad thing. No question about it.

Work it out . . . Me . . . If I *died*. That would worry me . . . The idea of being snuffed out . . . If I got *cancer*. That would worry me. Or if they stuck me in one of these concentration camps and one of Himmler's perverts got at me . . . That worries me . . . If Anne stopped loving me and ran off with another man . . . that would worry me.

I've got a whole scale of things that could worry me . . . The Jews and their problems . . . Yes, they are on it . . . but very far down, for Christ's sake . . . Way down the scale. That's not so good, the Jews being so low down on my anxiety scale.

Emotionally. Intellectually . . .

As an intellectual concept it's fairly high as a moral problem . . . The thing is, I am fundamentally a happy person . . . That's what it is . . .

That's the problem. I'm a happy person . . . Absolutely . . .

Leo is a young mathematician and Nobel Prize-winner. He has found the solution that will lead to the construction of the next generation of atomic bomb. Unable to cope with the enormity of his discovery, he takes a post at an English university and attempts to hide away. One day he meets Gilly, a brilliant young student, who has reached a similar set of conclusions . . . it is to her that he addresses this speech.

The Genius *by Howard Brenton*

Leo   I'm cold.

He wanders over to his jacket and puts it on as he speaks.

I did the same work in America. It hit me like it hit you. Pur – it – y. The
world in a grain of sand, under your fingernail? I had all that
innocence. Arrogance.

A silence.

Then I was on a beach. Californian holiday? Up came an individual
and sat down beside me. Blue eyes, the body of a surfer. The
Government, Gilly, the Government of A – mer – ik – a. And it began.

Gilly   What did?

A silence.

Leo   Everything. The threat in a smile. The offer of power. A lead role
in a cage.

He puffs his cheeks and blows out.

They wanted the work and they wanted me, for Uncle Sam, the free
world, for weapons research, for – a – bomb. That's what it means, the
tune you and I scrawled out with our ballpens. You describe how
something lives and dear old human kind will use your words to kill it.

He shakes his head.

Oh boy, the consequence of describing life is death?

He laughs.

I am not a hero. I am an American boy who wants to get fucked. I was
made for fame and sex not paranoia in a lonely room, out of my mind
that the 'phone is bugged. So I said – OK, no calculation is pure.
Therefore calculate no more. I gave up, Gilly. I closed down. I exiled
me into my own head. If you are shit scared of the damage you can do,
do nothing, eh?

A silence.

In the end they let me alone. And let me hide, here in England. Then
you walked out in the snow one morning.

The Suicide is a satirical play set in post-revolutionary Russia. Semyon, frustrated with his life, declares his intention to commit suicide. He is immediately bombarded by various political factions and private individuals who wish him to state that his suicide is an act on their behalf. In a moment of frustration Semyon decides to do away with himself instantaneously, thus foiling any other parties wanting to exploit his suicide.

The Suicide *by Nikolai Erdman*

Semyon   They don't believe me! They simply don't believe me! Even Maria doesn't believe me. All right. You'll be sorry. Yes you will, Maria. Where's the gun? Ah, here it is.

(He takes the gun.) Need to be quick about it though, without thinking, through the heart . . . that's instantaneous death.

(He puts the gun to his chest.) Instantaneous? What if it isn't? In the mouth. It's instantaneous in the mouth.

(He puts the gun in his mouth. Takes it out.) I'll count to three.

(He puts it in his mouth.) Waaa . . . Thaaa . . . Gaaa . . .

(He takes it out.) Better count to a thousand.

(He puts it back in his mouth.) Waaa . . . thaaa . . . gaaa . . . fth . . .

(He takes it out.) Should do it through the heart if I'm going to count.

(He puts the gun to his chest.) One, two, three, four, five, six, seven, eight, nine . . . Bit cowardly, counting up to a thousand. Need to be quick about it though, decisive . . . up to a hundred . . . and that's it. No . . . up to fifteen is quicker . . . right now too.

(He puts the gun to his chest.) One, two, three, four, five, six, seven, eight, nine, ten, eleven, twelve . . . thirteen . . . fourteen . . . Maybe I shouldn't count at all . . . in the mouth then.

(Puts gun in his mouth. Takes it out.) Where does the bullet come out? Here . . . the head . . . Pity about the head. Spoils the appearance. Better through the heart. Have to find it though. Where is it? Ah! Here! And here! And here! And here! What a huge heart . . . it's beating everywhere. And the way it's beating! It's going to explode. Good God! If I die of a heart attack I won't have a chance to shoot myself! I mustn't die, I must not die . . . I must live, live, live . . . so that I can shoot myself. Too late, too late . . . I can't breathe . . . A minute, give me one minute . . . Keep beating . . . keep on beating . . . It's stopped . . .

(The gun drops from his hand.) Too late, I'm dying . . . Who's this?

A young man is drowned in a boating accident. His death affects the lives of not only his best friend and his fiancée but the entire closed and suspicious community.

Evens makes a living gathering driftwood by the sea. Despised and feared by the village as a witch, he is in fact one of the sanest members of the community. In this speech he is talking to the best friend of the drowned man on the morning of the inquest.

The Sea *by Edward Bond*

Evens I believe in the rat. What's the worst thing you can imagine? The universe is lived in by things that kill and this has gone on for all time. Sometimes the universe is crowded with killing things. Or at any rate there are great pools of them in space. Perhaps that's so now. At other times it falls out that they've killed everything off, including each other of course, and the universe is almost deserted. But not quite. Somewhere on a star a rat will hide under a stone. It will look out on the broken desert and from time to time it will scatter out to feed on the debris. A shambolling, lolloping great rat – like a fat woman with shopping bags running for a bus. Then it scuttles back to its nest and breeds. Because rats build nests. And in time it will change into things that fly and swim and crawl and run. And one day it will change into the rat catcher. I believe in the rat because he has the seeds of the rat catcher in him. I believe in the rat catcher. I believe in sand and stone and water because the wind stirs them into a dirty sea and it gives birth to living things. The universe lives. It teems with life. Men take themselves to be very strong and cunning. But who can kill space or time or dust? They destroy everything but they only make the materials of life. All destruction is finally petty and in the end life laughs at death.

Gosforth, the local publican, is attempting to organize the annual village fête. The odds are stacked against him; the weather is bad, the sound system doesn't work, and the local dignitary who will open the fête has arrived early. Then Gosforth is told that he is about to become a father. . . . Gosforth has just bustled into the tent and is explaining the itinerary to the local celebrity and his companion.

Gosforth's Fête, (*from* **Confusions**)
by Alan Ayckbourn

Gosforth   We rented both these damn tents, you see. Didn't really open them up until today. Didn't have the space. When we do, we find half the guy ropes are missing off the main marquee – this one's safe enough – had to do an emergency job. Not a window left in the district with any sash cord.

He laughs.

Now, the curriculum goes as follows. Two-thirty p.m. we plan to kick-off. I'll give you a short introduction – needn't be too long – as soon as you've finished – up strikes the band – got them coming over from Hadforth – they should be here – why aren't they? – then if you can mingle about a bit if you don't mind a spot of mingling – have a go at bowling for the pig – just seen Fred Crake's trailer so the pig's arrived safely, thank God – roll a few pennies and all that sort of thing – then, at three-thirty – if you can stay till then – I hope you can – Second Little Pendon Wolf Cubs' P.T. Display, organized by Stewart Stokes – that should go on for about half-an-hour – four o'clock tea, courtesy Milly Carter and assorted ladies – four-thirty, soon as they've swallowed their biscuits – novelty races, fathers' race, mothers' race, three-legged grandfathers' race, all that sort of rubbish – five-thirty to six – final round-off with an organized sing-song with the Hadforth Band – has the Reverend managed to get the song-sheets run off? – ten pounds to a quid he hasn't – six o'clock all pack up, dismantle tents – seven-thirty all cleared away because old Swales wants the field back for his cows first thing in the morning. Hope you can stay for a bit of the fun.

Quaint Honour, written in 1958, is about homosexuality in public schools. Tully has seduced and fallen in love with a younger boy. He is both baffled and excited by the depth of feeling he is experiencing. They are discovered and Tully is expelled. The younger boy insists on also leaving the school but then rejects Tully's excited offer of love. Tully is talking to his lover, having just been rejected by him.

Quaint Honour *by Roger Gellert*

Tully   No; about bread – I dreamt I walked into a huge bakery – you know, with ovens, and racks covered with rolls and buns and cakes and all the pastry you ever saw in your life. Yes, that was it, and – and you were on duty there, in a white apron and a big silly white hat like a chef. I suppose you were the baker's boy.

Anyway, there was no one else; just this gentle roaring of the ovens, and a haze of flour, and the smell of new bread; it was gorgeous. So I walked up and down, looking at all the cakes and things. There were two enormous long tables right down the middle of the bakery, and lots of elaborate bits of pastry laid out on them, as if it was an exhibition or something, sort of showpieces. Pies like cathedrals, loaves like wheatsheaves – you know. Yes, it must have been an exhibition. I remember now, because there was a notice outside which said: THIS WAY TO THE SHOWBREAD.

Anyway, I don't know why, but I got up on one of the long tables and started doing place-kicks with these strange-shaped loaves and things that were laid out – trying to land them in an open furnace. You just stood there, and you didn't say a thing, but when I looked at you there were tears streaming down your face. I remember feeling sorry about that, but I was so determined to prove that I could get all these things into the fire, and they were going in so neatly, and burning like fury. And then . . . my God, yes, I saw you were holding a loaf in your hands – a small ordinary loaf – but in a way it was surprising, because, you know, it was the only one in the place that was just shaped like a loaf and nothing more, just a little white loaf – and it seemed incredible. And you were holding it as if you didn't want me to touch it. But I jumped down from the table and snatched it from you, and chucked it into the fire.

And suddenly I felt cold all over, and I felt I'd done something terrible, so I ran to the fire, and stretched my arm right into the middle to try and pull your heart out . . . I – I mean the loaf. It was there, but not burning, just lying there. And I closed my fingers round it, and as soon as I did that it burst into flames, and then I couldn't move, and I couldn't budge it an inch. Oh, God, I tugged and tugged, and it only burnt faster, and I saw my arm was burning too, and turning to ash, and dropping away in flakes. It didn't hurt. I couldn't feel a thing – but suddenly I gave up. I let go of the little loaf, and at once it stopped burning – just like that – it stopped. And I took my arm out of the fire, and it looked awful, it was so awful I shut my eyes —

And then I woke up, and my arm had gone to sleep because you were lying on it.

A faith healer, his wife and manager travel across Ireland playing one-night gigs in village halls. The couple have lost their child whilst on the road, which has placed a great pressure on their marriage.

Teddy is a Cockney. He adores both the faith healer and his wife but is a true showman and cannot resist pushing Frank into performing. This speech is taken from Teddy's monologue to the audience. The entire play consists of four monologues: two by the faith healer, one by his wife and one by Teddy.

Faith Healer *by Brian Friel*

Teddy   Let me tell you about two dogs I had once. Okay? One was a white poodle and she was so brilliant – I mean, that dog she knew what you were thinking about before you even thought about it yourself. Before I'd come home at night, d'you know what that dog would do? She'd switch on the electric fire, pull the curtains, and leave my slippers and a bottle of beer sitting there beside my chair. But put her in front of an audience – fell apart – couldn't do nothing. Right. Now the other dog he was a whippet. Maybe you remember him, Rob Roy, The Piping Dog?

Brief pause.

Well, it was quite a few years ago. Anyway, you see that whippet, he was fantastic. I mean to say, just tell me how many times in your life has it been your privilege to hear a three-year-old male whippet dog play 'Come Into The Garden, Maud' on the bagpipes *and* follow for his encore with 'Plaisir d'Amour'. Okay? Agreed. Sensational talent. Ambition? I couldn't stop him rehearsing. Morning, noon and night he'd sit there blowing the bloody thing and working them bellows with his back leg – all night long if I'd let him. That's all he lived for, being on top of the heap. And brains? Had he brains, that whippet? Let me tell you. I had that dog four and a half years, until he expired from pulmonary exhaustion. And in all that time that whippet couldn't even learn his name! I mean it. I mean apart from his musical genius that whippet in human terms was educationally subnormal. A retarded whippet, in fact. I'd stub my toe against something, and I'd say 'God!', and who'd come running to me, wagging his tail?

Harry is a middle-aged, single man who lives alone. As Christmas Day approaches he finds his loneliness increasingly intolerable. Depressed and desperate, he reviews his life. The play is a one-man show.

Harry's Christmas *by Steven Berkoff*

Time: Christmas. Place: A room. **Harry** *is counting his Christmas cards.*

Harry   Four, five, six. That's all. That's the lot . . . but there's some from last year . . . let's see.

Looks through last year's.

I could maybe add a couple . . . No you shouldn't do that . . . that's silly . . . to make it look better . . . who cares? But it looks a bit thin. YOU WORRIED WHAT PEOPLE MIGHT THINK? Yeeah! PEOPLE WHO MIGHT DROP IN, MIGHT THINK, POOR HARRY, NOT VERY POPULAR? Something like that yeah. LOOK AT THE SIX CARDS AND PITY YOU? Maybe, yeah maybe. THINK, WHAT HAS HIS LIFE BEEN – TO HAVE SO FEW CARDS? Maybe, yeah. WHO AND WHAT DOES HE MEAN TO THE WORLD? Christmas tells you . . . that you have sweet FA. Christmas says that's your standing in the world . . . you score six miserable Christmas cards . . . Christmas to make you feel like you don't exist . . . Christmas is like an avalanche coming . . . you want to run away, but you've nowhere to hide . . . I hate it . . . Nah! It's not so bad . . . that's average for the season. But if I don't get more than six I'll definitely add two from last year . . . maybe three. Ha ha, maybe I put up all last year's, nah, the last five years' and have a bonanza. Ha! Ha! Gee you're popular Harry! Why save them? They're nice though, some of them. They remind me. It's a piece of memory.

Looks at cards.

Mum and Dad, brother and aunty . . . one from work and two from . . . friends. Those two . . . not seen them for years . . . but every year they send a card and I send one back . . . so they know I'm still alive . . . and the message is always the same: 'Give us a ring sometime.' But I don't, because they don't want to hear from me . . . not really . . . but it's nice to rub the old memories up a bit and then they get a card back . . . but not before. I wait and if they miss a year then so will I. But they only missed one in the last ten years. I had moved so it got misdirected or lost or is still seeking me out . . .

Rents is a comedy set in Edinburgh which follows the experiences of two rent-boys as they search for security and love.

This speech is taken from the original monologue on which the play was based.

Rents *by Michael Wilcox*

Robert   I started hanging around when I was fifteen and once I
began to break through I had a crazy time for six months . . . I was
astonished at the sort of custom I had with all these men, coming all
over me in the most unlikely situations. Christ . . . if a guy took me to
the cinema, I'd go out to the bog with him during the advertisements
and let him screw me. Never got caught or anything . . . some of the
guys that came in must have realised what was going on . . . but they
just went blind to the whole business. Anyway . . . I just couldn't stop
myself. It wasn't the sex or the pleasure of it exactly . . . it was seeing a
grown man that I most likely despised getting that excited about me
. . . my body . . . and feeling the tension and the sweat of him when he
came . . . and his dejection as he cleaned himself up with bog roll after
. . . the fear in his eye. Hatred in me gave me my satisfaction . . . and
the power. I knew they were using me and didn't give a shit about me
and I wanted to be sure they paid for it one way or another. One man
punched me in the mouth when I laughed at him . . . I had more
respect for him after that and went with him a few times . . . which was
unusual.

For good times I went with younger men or lads of my own age . . . the
beauty and pain exploding inside me. Christ . . . that's something I've
lost now . . . I keep searching.

Billy is an Asian mature student at the L.S.E. Together with a young Asian boy from Hounslow he invades the local Woolworths, taking three white people hostage. As the police mount a siege on the shop it becomes clear that the motives of the captors are very mixed and this is as much a political and social act as it is a crime. He is talking to the very young Community policeman who has come to negotiate with him for the release of the hostages.

Trial Run *by Nigel Williams*

Billy   Oh if it were only you and me and him and her. If there were nobody outside the room. Or even nothing beyond the city. No sea to confuse the shoreline, no countries beyond what we owned ourselves, no misery complicating our misery, making it less and worse than it is. Look – you want to be a child. I can see it in your face. But you know far too much. You have a sophisticated little smile. Why. My Golly Gosh I'll tell you what you are . . . you're a sham . . . you're a faux-naïf you're a fake you're not a policeman at all you're a doll you're a model you're an excrescence you're a waste of time you're a trick policeman you're –

He's worked himself up enough to let go now.

YOU'RE A DISGRACE TO YOUR CLOTH! YOU HEAR?
THERE'S A WHOLE LOT OUTSIDE THIS ROOM! DON'T
FORGET THAT MR COMMUNITY POLICEMAN! DON'T
FORGET THAT THE NEXT TIME YOU PAT A BLACK GIRL
ON THE HEAD!

Close to him.

THERE ARE WOMEN QUEUING IN YOUR PORTS TO SEE
THEIR HUSBANDS! WOMEN WITH CHILDREN WHO ARE
DENIED THE 'SIMPLE AND NACH'RAL RIGHT' TO SEE
THEM! THERE ARE FAMILIES SEPARATED! THERE ARE
WOMEN MADE STATELESS AND MEN WHO LOSE THEIR
FAMILIES TO GRATIFY THE IGNORANT SENSIBILITIES
OF PEOPLE LIKE THIS AND THIS AND THIS! THERE IS
BUCKETFULS OF IT AND JUST YOU REMEMBER YOU
WEAR THE FUCKING UNIFORM OLD BOY! YOU WEAR
THE SAME UNIFORM WHY IT COULD BE HIS UNIFORM
OR IT COULD BE THE COSTUME WORN BY THOSE *CUNTS*
WHO STOOD MY WIFE UP AGAINST A WALL AND –

He stops, totally and eerily calm suddenly.

Look. It's obvious sahib that I'm having you on. Oh so obvious. I
probably haven't got a wife any more than you're a real policeman. I'm
probably making her up in order to titillate your cheap concern. I'm
not the sort of wallah to have a wife. I'm clearly not the marrying kind
oh my Golly Gosh no. Oh no by samosa I'm not do you see? I must be
lying because it's just too perfect isn't it this man running around with
a boy from Southall and his wife is in that shed in Southampton or
wherever it is being jumped up and down on by Customs Officers well
that's just too much of a coincidence wouldn't you say? That's entirely
unacceptable eh? After all coincidences rarely happen in rooms do
they? Or if they happen they happen to suit someone's convenience – to
tie in with someone's design, someone who wants someone damaged or
killed or . . .

Switches to parody Indian waiter voice.

Look it's pretty damn clear to me that I'm not from the Indian
sub-continent at all. I'm probably from the B.B.C. Light
Entertainment department. I'm probably blacked up you see. I'm an
English actor doing a funny voice eh. But hear this –

In genuine grief.

The mother of my children and my children are being kept in a big
stone shed near Heathrow Airport because there are certain . . .
difficulties. So is it any wonder that I imagine the craziest things. That
I have this urge to hurt back. That I dream about . . .

51

A group of young friends in a small German town, all of whom
are long-term unemployed, seek escape from the boredom and
depression of their lives by acting out the story of Amundsen's
journey to the South Pole.

Slupianek has assumed the persona of Amundsen himself,
finding it easier to communicate through the success of this man
rather than through his own personal feeling of failure. This
speech takes place at the end of the play when they have
attained the 'Pole'. Slupianek is told by his friends that they are
all either leaving Germany, have found work or are going to the
Job Centre to look for work. Slupianek cannot relinquish the
fantasy world he has established and compares a visit to the Job
Centre with exploring the Antarctic.

The Conquest Of The South Pole
by Manfred Karge

Slupianek   What on earth's keeping Bjaaland?

Seiffert is at the Job Centre again. He set off pretty early. He's still
bleary-eyed but wide awake and raring to go. The white-washed
vestibule. A notice board, rooms, floors, right, left, straight ahead. Go
straight ahead. Hold the course. Do I wander off to the right? No. To

52

the left? Don't wander off to the left, you're obsessed by the left, raving leftie. Straight ahead, for ever straight ahead. A block of ice. No, a staircase. To the first floor. Step by step. Watch out, crevasses in the ice. Is there a bridge of snow anywhere? The last step, the first floor. A glass door. A long, grey-black polished corridor. Fluorescent lights on the ceiling. Long wooden benches crammed full of penguins. Nothing but penguins sitting there, keeping quiet, their heads bowed. No space to sit down. Standing room only. Ahead, the door that meant hope. It's white, white. What's behind it? The South Pole. Is that where the Pole actually is? Really and truly, or only from the plane? Perhaps it's only a wall of ice. Sheer, unclimbable. What am I saying, unclimbable? What are my ice-pick and crampons for? Hacking out steps. Click click. Step by step. Breath comes in spasms. Freezes immediately on your fur and goggles. I can't see a thing any more. But still, on, on. Remove that curtain. It isn't your turn yet, yells a penguin. Paws off that curtain. A penguin leaves. A bit of a bench becomes free. On no account sit down, on no account. If you're sitting down you fall asleep and freeze to death, easy as pie. When's my turn? Be patient, it takes time, please be patient. A pink cloud. I fall asleep. God help me. I fall asleep standing up. How much time has passed? The door is open. Come in. Filing cabinets right and left. Don't lose your way. Straight ahead. Hold the course. Do sit down. No, I won't sit down, says Seiffert. Do you want me to freeze to death? We've got oil-heaters, portable. Would you like a coffee? Yes, coffee, says Seiffert, a gulp of hot coffee. To wash down the lump in my throat. And you are? Bjaaland, says Seiffert. Funny name. We haven't got that in our files. Well then, says Seiffert, Adams. Yes, Adams, says Seiffert, I'm called Adams. Why are you gaping? I, says Seiffert, and you must excuse me, am snowblind. I, says Seiffert, am a moose and snowblind. A snowblind moose. Ponies, says Seiffert, are in any case better than dogs. They have to be shot. Rosi, says Seiffert, got a slip made of seal-skin. I beg you, says Seiffert, on bended knees, for a job on an ice-breaker. On an ice-breaker? No, says Seiffert, with a nice baker. I demand, yells Seiffert, a job with a nice baker. Yes, I am perfectly calm, says Seiffert. Yes, says Seiffert, I will sit down. You've got to telephone, says Seiffert, I understand. Yes, says Seiffert, I understand. Yes, says Seiffert, I quite understand. Any minute now two nice men will appear, because I'm far too cold in this thin jacket, in all this ice and snow. Yes, says Seiffert, they are good friends. They, says Seiffert, have my best interests at heart. Yes, they have a lovely warm jacket for me. But I don't want it, yells Seiffert. What are windows for?

Barbarians is a trilogy of plays following the experiences of three East End teenagers as they leave school and try to find employment.

Jan has joined the Army and is about to go on a tour of duty in Northern Ireland. Although normally reticent about his past, the night prior to his departure he talks of his mother for the first time.

Barbarians *by Barrie Keeffe*

Jan   They laughed at me mum . . . destroyed her. They took away her bowels, to stop it spreading. The doctors did. They gave her a plastic bag, she hated it – the bag to urinate in. She hated it, she said it was like having a bath wearing a life belt. She used to sing in the pub, by the flats. She wanted a garden. We never had one in the flats. Never lived on the ground, me mum didn't. The pub had a garden. Sit there drinking her Dubonnet and lemonade. She used to sing at the pub at nights sometimes. They had turns and she'd get up and sing. Even when she was very ill. And one Saturday night she had this . . . she had this lovely voice, beautiful. When she sang 'Goodnight Irene', old women cried. She was a legend, her voice.

54

(He sings.) Irene, goodnight, Irene goodnight I'll see you in my dreams.

Pause. He begins to cry.

And this Saturday night, they had this dwarf comic. He told tall stories and jokes, made me mum laugh. He said – see, there used to be a lot of blacks in there, and so he told jokes about the blacks. They liked them, I mean – well, they had to like them.

Pause.

And when he went off the stage, they never took off the microphone. And it was still there, only about three and a half feet from the ground. They asked for a song and me Uncle Harold, he said to me mum: 'Give us a song, Elsie. And the other people, they all said: 'Give us a song, Elsie. And she said: 'O no, I can't.' And then they all started chanting: 'Elsie, give us a song.' And the man on the piano, called Charles, he started playing the beginning of 'Goodnight Irene' 'cause it was like her signature tune and eventually she got up and she was very overcome because of all the warmth and the pub was nice, with warmth and friendship. And she stood up and the drummer gave her the hand microphone and still they forgot the dwarf's microphone which was still standing right in front of my mum. And she put up her hand to stop everyone cheering and the piano player asked for hush and my mum said: 'I'm very overcome to know you all cared for me 'cause of the collection from the pub to send me flowers when I had my unfortunate operation . . .' And she was very err . . . moved. Moved. And in the quiet, there was this sound . . . this noise. Coming out of the loudspeakers. Because the dwarf's microphone was still switched on . . . it was standing about waist height to my mother. The sound of gushing water. The microphone picked up the sound of my mum passing water into her plastic bag. Everyone could hear it. Through the loudspeakers, the sound went on and some people they . . . they . . .

Pause.

And some people, some of the people . . .

Pause.

Laughed. They laughed.

He stops crying. Long silence.

That night at home, she got up out of bed and went to the bathroom and drank a pint of bleach. Which killed her.

Pause.

After that, it was very quiet at home. I went two nights every week to the Cadets and then . . . I signed up. I don't . . . talk about it much. When I had the medical, I didn't tell them about my mum . . . I thought it best to say 'natural causes'.

Rat In The Skull is set in a Paddington police station where a suspected Irish terrorist is held awaiting interrogation by an RUC officer. The play shows the distrust and dislike both between the two Irishmen and the British police of whom they are both 'guests'. The terrorist addresses this speech to the audience whilst alone in his cell.

Rat In The Skull *by Ron Hutchinson*

Roche Not a hand on me. The next two days, not a hand on me.
They must have been running buses, there was coppers coming in from
all over the place. I swear to God, there was even a couple who said
would I mind if they got married in the cell, they were that proud of me.
Or proud of having me, more than like, Michael Patrick de Valera
Demon Bomber Roche. I said no. You like your privacy. Not that there
was too much of that, with the formation teams of interrogators coming
in every hour, on the hour: hard man; soft man; 'Like a smack in the
gob?'; 'Like a fag or a woman?'; relays and queues of the bastards, and
as one falls dead with exhaustion it's out by the legs, and the next man,
please. And the barking at you, and the showing you snaps of bits and
pieces of what was left when the thing went up, and being told they'd
stuff you in a bin-sack and have you out of the chopper if it was up to
them, and hanging's too good, and the light left on all the time, and the
peering up your backside with the nightlight, and breakfast a mug of
cold tea the copper said he'd gobbed in, and every time you were left
alone whoever walked by the cell door felt he had to aim a kick at it; just
to say hallo –

Well I wouldn't have minded so much, but I was nothing like the
photy-fits.

I'm no oil-painting, God knows, and that was the case even before I
had the nose, lip and eye job done, but fair play, it was nothing like. It
was nothing like and I was saying nothing, and were they as pissed-off a
bunch of cops as ever knew they'd only the forensic to go on, and
though that was going to be enough they'd feel safer with a cough or
more. But still never a hand on me. And fair play, the Mick was being
stitched all ways up, by the book and down the line and not a foot put
wrong and I'm telling you there were twenty-five big ones coming up,
sure fire thing, the world was turning into iron bars for yours truly
Michael Patrick de Valera You-Know-The-Rest-Of-It Roche.
Banged-up, closed-down, one stitched Mick.

Seachange is set aboard a holiday cruise ship where both the imminent Falklands War and the memory of a soldier's death at Gallipoli in 1916 have a profound effect upon the passengers.

John, a playwright, is pursued by the ghost of his grandfather who insists that John must tell his story so that he can rest in peace.

Seachange *by Stephen Lowe*

John *(softly, as though telling a children's story)*   My grandfather was injured by a horse that ran wild at the landing at Gallipoli. Its belly had been ripped open by the barbed wire hidden under the surface of the water. Somehow, in all that carnage, his comrades got him on a Red Cross ship. He thought he was lucky, on his way back to Devon to recuperate. Heaven. But the ship was bombed, not far from here. It sank in a clear glass sea. It was not one of those stormy days that Ulysses beat his way through. Ideal holiday weather. Of course a Red Cross should not have been attacked. Geneva conventions. But both sides by this time had been running arms and fresh troops under its flag. His ship, however, was the real thing, not sailing under false colours, but he, and many others, had to pay the price for the deceit of generals as always. This much is known history.

He wipes his hands and face.

As the water poured into his ward, a nurse tried to calm him, although she must have been terrified herself. She wiped his sweat away, and gave him a sip of clear water. He thought this gesture absurd as the water rose around their feet. Absurd but . . . fine. He loved her so much in that moment that it hurt him more than his injury. She didn't try to escape, perhaps there was no escape, perhaps it never crossed her mind. That he'd never know, just as he would never know if anyone survived.

Pause.

As the first wave of water hit them, she'd freed his arms but not his legs. The screams of the dying men were deafening, echoing against the broken skin of the ship. He hung around her neck, holding on. The second wave covered them. They held their bursting breath, but that last air does not last into eternity. And so they gulped in the water, as though they'd wandered in from out of a desert. And he thought, in that torrent that so suddenly became a silent pool, he thought he could see tears trickling down her face. He knew this to be crazy, how could you see such a thing? With all that water around you?

He smiles.

And even if you could, even if there were tears, what did it matter to either of them, or to anybody else. They were dead, anyway.

59

Two arsonists move into a man's house and begin their preparations to raze it to the ground. The nearer they come to lighting the fire the more he attempts to befriend and placate them.

Beelzebub is revealed to be one of the fire raisers in the afterpiece when the man and his wife find themselves in heaven.

The Fire Raisers *by Max Frisch*

Beelzebub　My childhood faith! My childhood faith!

Thou shalt not kill, ha, and I believed it.

What are they making of my childhood faith!

The Figure cleans his finger nails.

I, the son of a charcoal burner and a gypsy woman, who couldn't read but knew the Ten Commandments off by heart, I'm possessed by the Devil. Why? Simply because I scorned all commandments. Go to hell, Joe, you're possessed by the Devil everyone said to me, and I went to hell. I lied, because then everything went better, and I became possessed by the Devil. I stole whatever took my fancy and became possessed by the Devil. I whored with whatever came my way, married or unmarried, because I had the urge to, and I felt fine when I gave way to my urge and became possessed by the Devil.

And they feared me in every village, for I was stronger than all of them, because I was possessed by the Devil. I tripped them up on their way to church, because I felt the urge, I set fire to their stables while they were praying and singing, every Sunday, because I felt the urge, and I laughed at their God who did not lay hold of me. Who felled the fir tree that killed my father in broad daylight? And my mother, who prayed for me, died of worry over me, and I entered the orphanage to set fire to it, and the circus to set fire to it, because I felt the urge more and more, and I started fires in every town simply in order to be possessed by the Devil. – Thou shalt! Thou shalt not! Thou shalt! Because we had no newspapers and no radio out there in the forest, we had only a Bible, and therefore I believed that one became possessed by the Devil if one killed and ravished and murdered and mocked every commandment and destroyed whole cities – that's what I believed! . . .

The Figure laughs.

It's no laughing matter, Willie!

It is Dennis's fortieth birthday. As his guests arrive, discussing the neighbourhood community programme and the mysterious attacks on garden gnomes, Dennis struggles to break out of his domesticity and find a new meaning to his life. Here he is talking to his friends after his birthday dinner about his pet dislikes.

One For The Road *by Willy Russell*

Dennis Every time I see a new piece of Tupperware in the house it feels like another little invasion has taken place . . . It seems to have a will of its own. I dreamt about it the other night. I dreamed that all the Tupperware in the house gelled together into one big plastic mass and began rollin' and slidin' up the stairs, on and on, through the bedroom door and sliding across the carpet, creepin' up onto the bed and pouncin' on me. The more I struggled, the more wrapped up in it I became until finally I stopped struggling and became The Tupperware Man. (. . .)

An' in the next part of the dream I was Tupperware Man himself – I could fly and everything I touched turned to Tupperware. The world was in a panic. They sent Superman after me, and Batman and Robin and Luke Skywalker and Wonder Woman. But they were all helpless in the face of Tupperware Man. I turned them all into Tupperware – Batman and Robin became a butterdish an' egg cup, Superman was turned into a picnic box, Luke Skywalker into a salad spinner an' I turned Wonder Woman into a huge, tit-shaped jelly mould. Planet Earth was in danger of becoming a Tupperware Globe when the Americans came up with a new invention – Tupperware Woman. They sent her after me and I tried to resist, but it was no good, I was helpless in the face of her. An irresistible force drew me towards her, I couldn't stop myself, I struggled to keep away from her but I was drawn on and on. Beaten, I gave up, I kissed her and me lid flew off. It was all over.

Being Friends is one of a trilogy of short plays about the profound effects of a chance meeting on the protagonists. The plays are thematically linked by the twentieth-century wars.

Oliver is a Quaker and a conscientious objector in the Second World War. He meets a young homosexual who has been kept out of the Army by a motorcar accident and they befriend one another. Oliver is working as a farmer. He is in his early twenties and comes from Manchester. Here he is explaining how he came to be involved in land work.

Being Friends *by Robert Holman*

Oliver   I didn't. In fact I started out in a hospital as a nurse's helper. At my tribunal that's what I asked for. It was very repetitive work. Maybe I haven't the right to say that?

A slight pause.

I don't want to make judgements on what I saw. I saw a lot of very ill men. Terrible injuries really, particularly the burns. They smell awful – the patient can smell himself.

There are only a few cherries left in the bottom of the bag. They have stopped eating them.

Then one day we had a German. I was asked to sit by him. They were very keen he didn't die. He had round-the-clock attention. No one else ever did.

A slight pause.

I think he'd been tortured. It looked to me very much like he had, he was in a terrible state. There was something unnatural about his injuries – can I say? It looked to me as if someone had pushed a needle into his eye. The cuts were very clean.

A slight pause.

I won't mention much else. It just looked to me as if a torturer had gone far too far. His fingers were missing. But I may be wrong.

A slight pause.

I wanted him to die. Which he did, thank the Lord. The anger unleashed on me. I went and told them I didn't want to work there any more.

A slight pause.

Spell #7 is written as a poetic piece reflecting the lives and experiences of black people in America. A group of performers meet in a bar to sing, dance and talk about their lives.

Eli is the bartender who listens to their problems. He is also a poet. In this speech he has just broken up a fight between two female dancers.

Spell #7 *by Ntozake Shange*

eli   people keep tellin me to put my feet on the ground
i get mad & scream/ there is no ground
only shit pieces from dogs horses & men who dont live
anywhere/ they tell me think straight & make myself
somethin/ i shout & sigh/ i am a poet/ i write poems
i make words cartwheel & somersault down pages
outta my mouth come visions distilled like bootleg
whiskey/ i am like a radio but i am a channel of my own
i keep sayin i write poems/ & people keep askin me
what do i do/ what in the hell is going on?
people keep tellin me these are hard times/ what are
you gonna be doin ten years from now/
what in the hell do you think/ i am gonna be writin poems
i will have poems inchin up the walls of the lincoln tunnel/
i am gonna feed my children poems on rye bread with horseradish/
i am gonna send my mailman off with a poem for his wagon/
give my doctor a poem for his heart/ i am a poet/
i am not a part-time poet/ i am not a amateur poet/
i dont even know what that person cd be/ whoever that is
authorizing poetry as an avocation/ is a fraud/
put yr own feet on the ground

The Accrington Pals are a battalion of men from Lancashire who are going over to fight in the trenches in the First World War.

Ralph has a carefree, expansive nature and rarely seems to take the war seriously. He is involved with Eva, a young woman whom he has left behind in Accrington. This is the letter he will never write to Eva; he is in the middle of a battle and knows his death is imminent.

The Accrington Pals *by Peter Whelan*

Ralph Oh my dearest, my own little pocket Venus . . . my rose of Clayton-le-Moors. This is no letter you'll ever get. My love. Sweet Eva. It's come. After God's long ages it's come and we're up to the line for the big push. But for the moment we're lost, as ever. Lost three times finding support trench. Now lost again. It's like a bake oven this summer night. I'm in a muck sweat. My sore throat's back. I've spewed my ring up twice. They say Jerry's beat but there's lads seen his observer balloons up all afternoon watching every move we made. I was ready enough once. Christmas when they sent us off to fuckin Egypt to fight Johnnie Turk. But he was whipped before we got there so I'd got myself ready for nowt. I was ready when they brought us back and into France. But it's been up and down, round and round, in and out, waiting and waiting till I don't know how I shall go at it. I've heard the flies buzzing out there. Every shell or bomb as falls short sends up clouds. Still, they're only old regulars lying out there, who, as May would say, are very low at the best of times. I've been a bastard to you Eva, if you only knew. Slept with whores. And one little mam'selle in Amiens who'd take no pay. I sat on her doorstep right after and cried for you. All I want to volunteer for now is a night raid on your bosom in a field of snowy white bedsheets. That's a fact.

The 'serious money' of the title refers to the fortunes to be made and lost working in the City on the Stock Exchange.

Zac is an American dealer working in Britain. He becomes involved in helping Scilla, another dealer, find the murderer of her brother but his motives are financial rather than compassionate. The play is written as a modern verse play in which every character's over-riding passion is for money.

Serious Money *by Caryl Churchill*

Zac   And the guy walked.
   (He walked with twenty million dollars but he walked.)

The financial world won't be the same again
Because the traders are coming down the fast lane.
They don't even know it themselves, they're into fucking or getting a
   Porsche, getting a Porsche *and* a Mercedes Benz.
But you can't drive two cars at once.
If you're making the firm ten million you want a piece of the action.
You know you've got it made the day you're offered stock options.
There are guys that blow out, sure, stick too much whitener up their
   nose.
Guy over forty's got any sense he takes his golden handshake and goes.
Because the new guys are hungrier and hornier,
They're Jews from the Bronx and spivs from South Carolina.
It's like Darwin says, survival of the fit,

Now, here in England, it's just beginning to hit.

The British Empire was a cartel.
England could buy whatever it wanted cheap
And make a profit on what it made to sell.
The empire's gone but the City of London keeps
On running like a cartoon cat off a cliff – bang.
That's your Big Bang.
End of the City cartel.
Swell.
England's been fucking the world with interest but now it's a different
   scene.
I don't mind bending over and greasing my ass but I sure ain't using
   my own vaseline.

Now as a place to live, England's swell
Tokyo treats me like a slave, New York tries to kill me, Hong Kong
I have to turn a blind eye to the suffering and I feel wrong.
London, I go to the theatre, I don't get mugged, I have classy friends,
And I go see them in the country at the weekends.

Road is an episodic play set in a street in Lancashire where unemployment and despair is rife. Throughout the play different characters reveal the state of their lives.

Skin is one of these characters. This speech is the only time Skin appears in the play. However, it is imperative to read the whole play to understand this character.

Road *by Jim Cartwright*

*Lights come up on a **Young Man** sitting on a wooden chair. A bare light bulb is dangling.*

Skin   Om. He opens his eyes. He sees you. He wants to tell you the story. He feels the need to drift back on the tide of his memory, back, back, back. And I'm the lonely skinhead again. Jogging away, every day, to be the best, to be the best. And the press-ups. And the sit-ups. And the 1-2-3, 1-2-3, 1-2-3, 1-2-3. And you've gotta be fit to fight, and I do, every Saturday night, with my friends at weekends, fight. Do you know about fighting? No. I'll tell you in my story. And I want to be the best skinhead and I want to give everything, every single thing, to the experience of the tingle. I'll tell you about the tingle later. And you've got to be fit to fight, and practise tactics every night.

(He practises on an imaginary opponent.) Do you? I do?

(Practises.) Do you work in the asbestos factory? I did.

(Practises. Stops.) I'll explain.

He indicates the imaginary opponent.

My opponent! Anyone you like! City fan, the cunt that shagged Ricky's bird, Ted the Foreman, you choose. Targets!

Goes down on imaginary body.

Face, neck, beerbag, dick, shin, top of the foot. Today I want the neck, this vein here. I don't want to fuck Christine Dawson, I don't want my mother's love. I don't want to work at the engineering firm, I want the neck, this vein here.

(Practises.) Tactics, new techniques. What does he think? What do you think?

(Strikes.) You thought, he thought, the neck and that's that. The neck and that is that. Now I've told you about the three things you need to get to the experience of the tingle. One, fitness, told you. Two, tactics, told you. Three, new techniques, I told you. Now I'll tell you about the tingle.

He comes off the stage into the audience. This next bit should be improvised.

Well it's . . . you can't say it, can you . . . ? It'll come when you're fighting. Sometimes in the middle, sometime beginning, sometime end, but it won't stay . . . it's like you are there, you are fighting, but 'you' are not there . . .

Pause.

You don't understand.

Pause.

Anyway, once you've had it you need it, and I thought that's all there was until that night, right, should I tell you about that night? No. I'll show you.

He leaps back on stage.

I came out the disco, last man to leave, all my lads had gone. I'd been talking to Mickey Isherwood the bouncer.

'See you Jim.'

'Aye, see you Ishey.'

Then I saw them. Skins. Bolton boot-boys. Skinheads. Some sitting on the wall, some standing. I moved off to the right.

'Eh, cunty.'

'Eh, git head.'

'Come 'ere.'

I looked at the moon. I heard the crack of denim, the scuffle down the wall, the pad and fall of the Dr Martins, pad, pad, pad. I closed my eyes. Pad, pad. As they moved in, pad, pad. I moved out. Pad, pad. I felt their breath . . . lifted one man by the chin . . . can you imagine it? Magnificent . . . they were scattering. Caught one man between thigh and calf, took him round to the ground, fingers up the nose, dragged a pace, nutted, lifted my fingers to pierce out his eyes when, to my surprise, I saw a figure watching, like a ghost, all pale in the light. He was laughing at me. Mocking my whole fucking life. I sprang; when I arrived, he'd gone. Too quick for me? No, I saw him disappear down a blind alley. I had him now. I had him now!

He was facing the wall in a sort of peeing position. I moved in to strike, my fist was like a golden orb in the wet night, I said it was night, I struck deep and dangerous and beautiful with a twist of the fist on the out. But he was only smiling, and he opened his eyes to me like two diamonds in the night. I said it was night, and said, 'Over to you, Buddha.'

Pause.

So now I just read the dharma. And when men at work pass the pornography, I pass it on and continue with the dharma. And when the man on the bus pushes I continue with the dharma.

Om.

Teendreams follows the lives of two women, showing how their teenage idealism of the sixties is eroded by the experiences of being a wife, mother and teacher in the seventies.

Kevin is in his early twenties. He is acting as best man at the wedding of Howard and Rosie; this is his best man speech.

Teendreams *by David Edgar and Susan Todd*

Kevin Right. Oh, first of all, it falls on me, on your behalf, to express our thanks to the bridesmaids and the pageboy. That's the bridesmaids there, and the pageboy there. Luckily it's quite easy to tell them apart. Usually nowadays to tell the boys from the girls you need a search warrant. But, uh . . . . Anyway.

Oh, darlings, I don't know which of you got the bouquet, but could you hand it in, 'cos the man with the window box next door is screaming for it back.

Well, all I can say is, if I've got the right joke here, yes, all I can say is it's a good thing it's not a Scottish wedding. I mean, I went to one last week, and it's the only wedding I been to where the confetti's on elastic.

Anyway, the happy couple. Well, I known 'em, haven't I? Known Howard since he was that high (*very low*). Last Thursday, and Rosie since she was that high (*rather high*). And I know Howard's always wanted someone to look up to . . . not to mention Rosie wanting someone to look down on . . .

Sorry, How, Rosie, had to slip that one in, as the Art Mistress said to the Gardener, sorry, the other way round . . .

Please yourselves.

Well, anyway, I s'pose I better, enough of this merry badinage . . . the first uh, telegram. . . . To Howard and Rosemary, first telegram:

'Note Merged Accounts Stop Future Products Filed In Pending Query Hope Not Triplicate Congrats From All At Office.'

Well, now i'n't that nice. The second telegram, from Frances, 'Don't', I s'pose that's 'Don't . . . forget your promises love Frances', dunno quite what that means, Rosie? Eh? The third –

Blackout on **Kevin**.

Henry is a playwright married to Annie who is an actress. They have both walked out of marriages to be with one another. They are desperately in love but is it the Real Thing? In this speech Henry is talking to his daughter who is about to go travelling with her fairground lover.

The Real Thing *by Tom Stoppard*

Henry It's to do with knowing and being known. I remember how it stopped seeming odd that in biblical Greek 'knowing' was used for making love. Whosit 'knew' so-and-so. Carnal knowledge. It's what lovers trust each other with, knowledge of each other, not of the flesh but through the flesh, knowledge of self, the real him, the real her, *in extremis*, the mask slipped from the face. Every other version of oneself is on offer to the public. We share our vivacity, grief, sulks, anger, joy . . . we hand it out to anybody who happens to be standing around, to friends and family with a momentary sense of indecency perhaps, to strangers without hesitation. Our lovers share us with the passing trade. But in pairs we insist that we give ourselves to each other. What selves? What's left? What else is there that hasn't been dealt out like playing cards? A sort of knowledge. Personal, final, uncompromised. Knowing, being known. I revere that. Having that is being rich. You can be generous about what's shared – she walks, she talks, she laughs, she lends a sympathetic ear, she kicks off her shoes and dances on the tables, she's everybody's and it don't mean a thing, let them eat cake. Knowledge is something else, the undealt card, and while it's held, it makes you free and easy and nice to know, and when it's gone, everything is pain. Every single thing. Every object that meets the eye, a pencil, a tangerine, a travel poster. As if the physical world has been wired up to pass a current back to the part of your brain where imagination glows like a filament in a lobe no bigger than a torch bulb. Pain.

Woza Albert attempts to show one particular view of what would happen if Christ came to South Africa. It is a two-hander in which each actor plays a variety of parts ranging from brick makers to the white President of South Africa. At this point Mbongeni is playing an old man being interviewed for the television cameras. Morena is Jesus.

Woza Albert *by Mtwa/Ngema/Simon*

Mbongeni *(speaking)*   Eh? What would happen to Morena if he comes to South Africa? What would happen to Morena is what happened to Piet Retief! Do you know Piet Retief? The big leader of the white men long ago, the leader of the Afrikaners! Ja! He visited Dingane, the great king of the Zulus! When Piet Retief came to Dingane, Dingane was sitting in his camp with all his men. And he thought, 'Hey, these white men with their guns are wizards. They are dangerous!' But he welcomed them with a big smile. He said, he said, 'Hello. Just leave your guns outside and come inside and eat meat and drink beer.' Eeeeii! That is what will happen to Morena today! The Prime Minister will say, just leave your angels outside and the power of your father outside and come inside and enjoy the fruits of apartheid. And then, what will happen to Morena is what happened to Piet Retief when he got inside. Dingane was sitting with all his men in his camp, when Piet Retief came inside. All the Zulus were singing and dancing . . . Bamya-lo-Kandaba payimpi . . .

Repeats snatches of the song.

And all the time Dingane's men were singing and dancing,

Proudly.

they were waiting for the signal from their kind. And Dingane just stood up. . . . He spit on the ground. He hit his beshu and he shouted, Bulalan 'abathakathi. Kill the wizards! Kill the wizards! Kill the wizards! And Dingane's men came with all their spears.

Mimes throat-slitting, throwing of bodies.

Suka! That is what will happen to Morena here in South Africa. Morena here?

Disgusted.

Eeii! Suka!

Hugo is twenty-one and French. An intellectual, he has begged to be allowed a more physical role in the Communist Party and has been assigned the job of assassinating a suspected traitor. He finds himself caught between his growing admiration for his victim and his frustration at not being accepted by the less intellectual members of the Party.

Les Mains Sales *by Jean-Paul Sartre*
(from *The Assassin* trans. Frank Hauser)

Hugo For once you're right, comrade. I don't know the meaning of appetite. If you'd seen the tonics of my childhood: I left half of them — what a waste! So they opened my mouth and they said 'One spoonful for papa, one spoonful for mama, one spoonful for Aunt Anna.' And they shoved the spoon right down my throat. And I grew, can you believe. But I didn't get any fatter. That was when they made me drink blood fresh from the abattoir, because I was a bit pasty: since when I've never touched meat. Every evening my father would say 'That child isn't hungry.' Every evening, you can see it from here: 'Eat, Hugo, eat. You'll make yourself ill.' They made me take cod liver oil. That's the height of luxury: a drug to make you hungry, while in the streets there were those who would have sold themselves for a steak, I saw them pass by my window with their placards: 'Give us bread.' And I sat down at table. Eat, Hugo, eat. One spoonful for the doorman who's out of work, one spoonful for the old woman gathering scraps from the dustbin, one spoonful for the carpenter's family, the carpenter who's broken his leg. I left home. I joined the Party to hear the same old song: 'You've never been hungry, Hugo, what are you interfering for? What can you understand? You've never been hungry.' Well, then, no, I've never been hungry. Never! Never! Never! Perhaps *you* can tell me what I've got to do to stop you all blaming me for it.

Bloody Poetry follows the lives of the poets Byron and Shelley over three summers in the early nineteenth century. The poets travel through Europe, writing, arguing and making love with their wives and mistresses.

Polidori is Byron's personal physician. He feels himself to be an object of scorn and amusement to the two couples and resents them bitterly.

Bloody Poetry *by Howard Brenton*

Polidori   I entered the drawing-room of the Villa Diodati. Outside,
there raged the storm. No. Outside the storm raged. No. Outside, the
storm abated. No. Outside, the storm I had just left, rolled around the
gloomy house. No. No. I was wet and miserable.

He looks around the group. **Byron** *and* **Claire** *kiss passionately.* **Mary** *shifts
towards* **Bysshe,** *turning the pages of the Wordsworth. They do not respond to*
Polidori *'s presence.*

In a flash I saw them, a flash of lightning. The air in the room was
heavy with their illicit sexuality, they had been at it, I knew it! I knew
it! I knew it! They had thrown their clothes back on, the minute I came
to the door! No. The two great poets, were, I observed in
contemplation, the women observing a discreet silence.

Mary turns, she and **Bysshe** *kiss passionately.* **Polidori** *flinches.*

No. The profligate would-be-poets and their, their whores, lounged
upon the floor, and felt disgraced at my entrance, for I brought with me
the wind and the rain.

He looks from couple to couple.

No. I am so lonely. Why do they assume I am second rate, when I am,
not! When I am not second rate? I mean has Shelley ever had a good
review in his life? As for my life, I have never done one thing that is not
decent, to anyone; or going on middling to decent! And look at them.
Byron is an overweight alcoholic, Shelley is an anorexic, neurotic mess!
The planet is bestrewn with their abandoned children, lovers of both
sexes and wives! Shelley has tuberculosis, Byron has syphilis and these
are the men whom the intelligent among us worship as angels of
freedom. No. It was a privilege to be the friend of those two young,
beautiful men, in the heyday of that summer. No. Yes. After all, I am
paid five hundred pounds, by Byron's publisher, to write a diary of this
summer. Dreadful time, no! Time of my life. My decent life. So!

The couples finish their kisses.

I entered the living-room of the Villa Diodati, that stormy night.

Bernard is a successful English lecturer. He moves into a new house but finds his life becomes affected by the previous owner, Haggerty, and the problems he has left behind.

Bernard regularly visits his elderly father. He struggles to communicate genuinely but more often than not falls prey to frustration and anger.

After Haggerty *by David Mercer*

Bernard   Dad – who can resist you? Who can resist a man who writes: 'Your Uncle Charlie's had his other leg off. A finer man never wore a pair of boots'? *(Pause.)* Look, I'm only trying to say the statement has its comic side. *(Pause.)* I *know* there's nothing funny about losing both your legs. For God's sake! *(Pause.)* Look, I was in the bloody, blasted war, you know! *(Pause.)* What? *(Pause.)* I've told you before. I got that wound in the arse when I was climbing out of a burning tank! It's not, cowardice-wise, a question of which way I was pointing, dad. *(Pause.)* How could I be running away from the Germans when the sods had us encircled? Go on! Tell me! And tell me, whilst we're at it, why you have to bring it up about three times a year? *(Pause.)* You've given me more scars talking about it than the actual piece of bloody shrapnel! *(Pause.)* I *know* it's not the same as Uncle Charlie. So he gets one chopped off down the pit, and one sawn off years later in hospital. I mean, I suppose the surgeon knew what he was doing. I just – *(Long pause.)* All right. I'll accept that. We'll try to stay off 'controversial topics'. Jesus. *(Long pause.)* Dad, you don't believe in God either so why get worked up about me saying Jesus? *(Long pause.)* Yes, I expect I am a bit tanned. I've been in Cuba. I wrote and told you I was *going*. All I can say is your memory for anything to do with me has *gone*. It simply doesn't function. *(Long pause.)* Well, I was a bit frightened of sharks. Sea's boiling with sharks round there. *And* barracuda. *(Long pause.)* Three and a half pounds, was it? A perch? Down at Crawston Dam. *(Pause.)* Dad. Don't say things like: 'From the sublime to the ridiculous'! Please. There is *no* contest on between my sharks and your perch. None whatsoever. *(Long pause.)* What? You thought Cuba was part of America and it's been and gone and gone communist?

Bernard stands, looking in front of him woodenly. Long pause.

Dad. Your mind doesn't have ideas. It has enigmatically related confusions. *(Pause.)* Sorry. *(Pause.)* I was about to say there was a sense in which Cuba was part of the USA. But it bloody well isn't any more. *(Long pause.)* Why are you crying? *(Pause.)* All my life I thought you were something like a mute. *(Pause.)* She did all the talking. *(Pause.)* Now *you* do the talking. *(Pause.)* And when you revert. When you go mute. Which is to say: when I begin to think I recognize you again – dammit, you cry! *(Long pause.)* Padre o muerte! Venceremos!

Moving Pictures is set in Nottingham in the 1960s and follows the lives of two families. In one a son watches as his adored mother is dominated by his father. In the other a gentle man is forced towards mental breakdown by his overpowering wife.

Pete is the son of the latter family. He is a young clerk and in this speech describes his feelings after his mother and father have arrived at the dole office, where he works, asking for money.

Moving Pictures *by Stephen Lowe*

Pete *(distressed)* It was just seein' 'em both, I suppose. The other side of the glass. It's bad enough when it's folk you don't know, come cap in hand, but when it's me own mam and dad. He thought we were the bookies. He kept scrawling names of horses on the forms, and sliding 'em under the glass. Grinnin' away. He din't know who I was. When I saw her come into the office, draggin' him like a dog on a lead, I just din't know . . . (. . .)

Silence.

She din't come to tell me. She'd been round the Panel screamin' blue murder at them stoppin' his money. Then she'd come straight round to us, to see what we had goin'. She saw me as a soft touch. She went up the bloody wall when I told her what the rate was. I mean, I can't work miracles. I wish I could. I should have done someat for him. There's nought I could do. I feel such a failure. He looked so bloody lonely.

I kept catchin' me face in the glass when I looked at 'im. I'll end up like 'im. I know I will.

Translations is set in Ireland in the early nineteenth century. Yolland is an English soldier who has come to make the first Ordnance Survey. For the purpose of the map the original Gaelic names have to be changed to English. This simple administrative act has a profound effect upon the Irish locals and Yolland himself.

His interpreter is Owen, an Irishman who left the hedge-school and the community to live in Dublin for six years. Yolland is speaking to Owen whilst Owen works on the translation.

Translations *by Brian Friel*

Yolland Father has that drive, too; that dedication; that indefatigable energy. He builds roads – hopping from one end of the Empire to the other. Can't sit still for five minutes. He says himself the longest time he ever sat still was the night before Waterloo when they were waiting for Wellington to make up his mind to attack. (. . .)

Born in 1789 – the very day the Bastille fell. I've often thought maybe that gave his whole life its character. Do you think it could? He inherited a new world the day he was born – the Year One. Ancient time was at an end. The world had cast off its old skin. There were no longer any frontiers to man's potential. Possibilities were endless and exciting. He still believes that. The Apocalypse is just about to happen . . . I'm afraid I'm a great disappointment to him. I've neither his energy, nor his coherence, nor his belief. Do I believe in fate? The day I arrived in Ballybeg – no, Baile Beag – the moment you brought me in here, I had a curious sensation. It's difficult to describe. It was a momentary sense of discovery; no – not quite a sense of discovery – a sense of recognition, of confirmation of something I half knew instinctively; as if I had stepped . . . (. . .)

No, no. It wasn't an awareness of *direction* being changed but of experience being of a totally different order. I had moved into a consciousness that wasn't striving nor agitated, but at its ease and with its own conviction and assurance. And when I heard Jimmy Jack and your mother swopping stories about Apollo and Cuchulainn and Paris and Ferdia – as if they lived down the road – it was then that I thought – I knew – perhaps I could live here . . .

Now embarrassed.

Where's the pot-een? (. . .)

Poteen – poteen – poteen. Even if I did speak Irish I'd always be an outsider here, wouldn't I? I may learn the password but the language of the tribe will always elude me, won't it? The private core will always be . . . hermetic, won't it?

Insignificance shows modern man's attempts to come to terms with his own mortality in the face of the nuclear threat. Four legends of Fifties America meet in a hotel room one night. The Ballplayer, loosely based on Joe DiMaggio, suspects his wife (Marilyn Monroe) of being unfaithful to him. In this speech he is talking to the Professor (Einstein) whilst waiting for his wife to come out of the bathroom.

Insignificance *by Terry Johnson*

Ballplayer Some punk kid thinks he's a bigshot, they put him on a bubble gum card.

He throws it away.

You know how many bubble gum series I been in? Thirteen. Thirteen series. I been in Chigley's Sporting Greats. I been in Pinky's World Series Stars 1936, 1937, 1939, 1942, 1944, 1945, 1949 and 1951. I been in Tip Top Boy's Best Baseball Tips showing how best to pitch, swing, deadstop and slide, and I have been Hubbly Bubbly's Baseball Bites best all-rounder nine years running. So no, hey! Hold on. That's 13 series but . . . 21 separate editions all told. And how many kids you know collect? Card for card it must run into millions. I must be stuck in albums from here to the Pacific. World wide. They give gum to little Chink kids, don't they? You liberate them one day, next day they're making swops. I saw on TV they don't take beads and stuff up the Amazon no more; they take instant coffee and bubble gum. I could go into a little village in Africa that's hardly seen a white man and they'd say 'Hi Big Hitter, sit down and have some coffee.' This fame thing's enough to give you the heebies, I can tell you. Chigleys, Pinkys, Hubblys and Tip Top. That's some bubble gum.

A group of English people volunteer to work on a kibbutz hoping for sun and sex. For the Israelis the aims of the kibbutz are quite different. As the two sides attempt to work alongside one another their cultural differences become marked.

Mike has begun an affair with a kibbutznik. He has come to the kibbutz to find himself while she is serving her last year of military service on the kibbutz. Here Mike is explaining to her why he walked out of Cambridge.

Not Quite Jerusalem *by Paul Kember*

Mike   And I walked. I just kept walking. Walking and walking in the pissing rain. I just walked. Nothing momentous. No dead birds fell from the trees. No portents. I just walked, all the way along Trumpington Road.

Pause.

I got as far as Grantchester and I thought, fuck it, yes, why not? Do it. The heart of England trip. Get in touch with the true essence of England, what it is to be English. Let the village atmosphere seep into your pores. See if you can make contact with it, this magical thing called Englishness. I wanted to see if I could experience it. The place was deserted. I kept walking, past the old mill right up around the bend to where the council property starts and I thought oh, shit, council houses. I'm never going to find the spirit of true Englishness there. So I headed back to the village. Looked at all the usual things; the cottages, the rectory and so on and, eventually, as always, ended up in the churchyard; the one where people sometimes presume Rupert Brooke is buried? And there's the poem about the clock stopping? And it's all so wonderful and idyllic. And I was scouting around, vaguely aware that, in fact, I'd located it. The English idyll. That this essence of Englishness was actually there, in my possession. . . . And suddenly I caught sight of this . . . prat sailing down the Cam back towards Cambridge in a punt, with his girl doing all the work, while he reclined at the exact angle, trying to play a chord and strum a tune. . . . There was this idiot, sailing along, desperately trying to simulate an atmosphere of . . . Christ knows. Some vague recollection of tranquillity from his grandfather's scrapbook. It was all there. The spires in the background, the river, this typical English village and this prat; this arch tit, sailing through the stillness of centuries, absolutely fucking clueless.

Pause.

I walked out of the village, got to the main road, turned right instead of left and here I am. How do you put that in a letter?

Pause.

Are you any wiser?

This play looks at four young people who are deemed 'lucky' because they have employment in the City.

Dave is a young and intelligent Cockney. He is frustrated by the pettiness and hierarchy of the rat race.

The Lucky Ones *by Tony Marchant*

Dave D'you want to know what life's biggest mystery is? (D'you want to hear a bit of philosophy?) Why is it, I often find myself wondering, that you can never get a bar of chocolate out of a vending machine? I mean, wherever I go, especially on railway platforms, I see people innocently putting their 20p's in the slot in return for a bar of whole nut. And do they get it? Do they fuck. (The world is full of vending machine victims. They frown and tug at the bit that's supposed to pull out but it always seems to have been stuck with superglue or something.) So naturally they try to retrieve their coins by pushing the refund button but the machine only seems to think it's been designed to swallow your money. It doesn't seem to realize it was intended to provide anyone with chocolate. (Anyway), some people pluck up enough courage to give the machine a bang, but furtively – like reluctant vandals. Then they get embarrassed and go all red when other people start to look and they have to walk sheepishly away, having lost their 20p and their dignity. And their train has long gone while they, in their idealistic and pathetically hopeful way, thought they could persuade the machine to hand over the chocolate that they've paid for. Tough tits, says the machine, I've got your money, suckers, but you ain't having my whole nuts. (Some people smash the machine to bits but they get arrested.) Some people are luckier and manage to negotiate a packet of Wrigleys which is not what they wanted at all (but they're thankful for whatever the machine is kind enough to let them have). I've seen people with their arms pulled out of their sockets, slumped and sobbing beside vending machines, broken by the struggle, shame and deep shock of it all. Life is like a vending machine I reckon – out of order but with no sign up to warn you.

Cries From The Mammal House is an allegorical tale of a zoo facing bankruptcy. The only animal capable of restoring the zoo's fortunes is a creature as fantastic as the dodo.

Dave is a passionate conservationist. He balances a child-like delight in saving endangered species with a sardonic Welsh wit. Here he is talking to his local helper whom he believes has no knowledge of English.

Cries From The Mammal House
by Terry Johnson

Dave The Pink Pigeon is the perfect example of natural selection at
its worst. The real problem with breeding them is that they don't
bloody like one another. Thanks to you we've now got six potential
breeding couples; thirty-six possible combinations and no two of them
can bear to stand on the same bloody branch, let alone fornicate. And
look at that. Call that a nest? Call that a nest, you miserable bloody
thing? And there's not one of them learnt that the only kind of egg you
lay from a perch twelve feet above the ground is a scrambled one!
They're the stupidest bloody species I've ever come across. As for this
one, look at him. He's a pedigree bloody pigeon him, look. Pink as you
like, but he's only tried to mate once in three weeks; and that was with
his water dish. Come on boyo, make an effort. It's the survival of your
species we're talking about. They think I'm mad. Who does he think he
is, they say. We don't want to fuck. We don't like it. My mum and dad
were decent, they never fucked, so why should I? They think I'm mad.
I think I'm mad. Sometimes I wish you spoke English.

Jack Johnson was the first black man to win the Heavyweight Championship of the World. The play, based on his life, shows a man facing choices and temptations in the face of vindictive racism.

Scipio is a fantastical street philosopher. He addresses this speech directly to the black members of the audience just after Jack has been arrested for making love with a white woman.

The Great White Hope *by Howard Sackler*

Scipio   so Ah says good evenin to em, then Ah askin em this:
How much white you up to? How much you done took on?
How much white you pinin for? How white you wanna be?
Oh, mebbe you done school yourself away fum White Jesus —
but how long you evah turn your heart away frum WHITE!
How you lookin, how you movin, how you wishin an figgerin —
how white you wanna be, that whut Ah askin!
How white you gaunta get — you tell me!
You watchin that boy? Nothin white-y bout him, huh?
But whut he hustle after? White man's sportin prize!
Whut he gotta itch for? White man's poontang?
Whut his rich livin like? White man's nigger!
Thinks he walkin and talkin like a natchul man,
don' know how he's swimmin half-drownded in the whitewash,
like they is, like you is, nevah done diffrunt,
gulpin it in evvy day, pickled in it, right at home dere —
tell me that ain't how we living!
Tell me how it better you chokin on dat whitewash
than wearin a iron colluh roun you neck!
Oh, yeah, you sayin, but whut kin we do,
Whut kin us or dat boy or dem gospellers do,
we passin our days in de white man's world — well,
make you own, brothers!
Don' try an join em an don't try an beat em,
leave em all at once, all together,
pack up!
Colleck you wages, grab whutevah here gonna come in handy
an sluff off de ress! Time to get goin!
Time again to makes us
a big new wise proud dark man's world
again! Ah says again! Ah tellin what we had once!
Nevah mine that singing — learn, brothers, learn! (...)
dat laughin don' harm us none!
Five hundrid million of us not all together,
not matchin up to em, dat what harmin us!
Dream bout it, brothers —
Five hundred million on dey own part of de earth,
am not a one dere evah asking another,
How much white you up to,
how white you wanna be ...

Glaring, he makes his exit.

The Art Of Success is set in Hogarth's London where corruption, dissolution and disease are rife. In this climate Hogarth is struggling to ensure a copyright on his engravings.

Walpole is the Prime Minister and controls the entire government by taking most public offices himself or giving them to members of his family. In this speech he is trying to write a play, having just made love to the Queen.

The Art Of Success *by Nick Dear*

An apartment in a palace. A large, ornate bed. A woman lies in it. **Walpole,** *half-dressed, sits at a nearby table, writing. He screws up a sheet of paper and throws it away.*

Walpole   It's not as easy as I thought. The costume changes are a bugger. I need the heroine half-naked for the climax, so I've got to find a reason to get her off-stage and then I've got to find another reason to get her on-stage again. Give me the House of Commons any day.

He looks to the woman.

I know it won't be a popular law. But hang me a booming economy seems to breed subversion more than an age of hardship. It is precisely the popularity of the playhouses that renders them such a threat. Oh, I long to bring in a sensible, modern system, in which it is simply made plain to these chaps that it's in their own interests to toe the Lord Chamberlain's line. . . . A hint here. . . . A whisper there. . . . Get the Artistic Director in for a cup of tea, wave a small cheque in his face. . . . Just nudge the idea in. Where did the thinking spring from, that art must necessarily equal trouble? I am pacific, it is my nature, I believe with all my heart that what we need for the growth of the nation is peace. I don't like trouble and nor do the people. We like a quiet life and a decent dinner and why can't these toe-rags accept it? – Ah! Good!

He writes fast.

Get your costume off, you difficult old bag.